*quizzes to find out if
he's right for you*

he loves me
he loves me not

barb karg

Adams media
avon, massachusetts

Published by
Adams Media,
an F+W Publications Company
57 Littlefield Street
Avon, MA 02322
www.adamsmedia.com

ISBN-10: 1-59869-458-8
ISBN-13: 978-1-59869-458-1

Printed in the United States of America.

J I H G F E D C B A

**Library of Congress Cataloging-in-
Publication Data**
Karg, Barbara.
He loves me, he loves me not / Barb Karg.
p.   cm.
ISBN-13: 978-1-59869-458-1 (pbk.)
ISBN-10: 1-59869-458-8 (pbk.)
1. Women—Psychology. 2. Man-woman
relationships.
3. Dating (Social customs) 4. Mate
selection. I. Title.
HQ1206.K368 2007
646.7'7082—dc22   2007030949

This publication is designed to provide
accurate and authoritative information with
regard to the subject matter covered. It is sold
with the understanding that the publisher is
not engaged in rendering legal, accounting,
or other professional advice. If legal advice
or other expert assistance is required, the
services of a competent professional person
should be sought.
—From a *Declaration of Principles* jointly
adopted by a Committee of the American
Bar Association and a Committee of
Publishers and Associations

Many of the designations used by manufac-
turers and sellers to distinguish their prod-
uct are claimed as trademarks. Where those
designations appear in this book and Adams
Media was aware of a trademark claim, the
designations have been printed with initial
capital letters.

*This book is available at quantity discounts
for bulk purchases. For information, please
call 1-800-289-0963.*

To **RICK**, my knight
in shining armor.

To the **BLONDE BOMBSHELL**,
the quintessential
Princess of Darkness.

And to **ALL WOMEN** who are
on the hunt for Mr. Perfect.
He's out there somewhere,
ladies, you just have to kiss
a lot of frogs to find him.
Godspeed to you all!

contents

acknowledgments

Creating a book is never a simple process. It takes many hard-working individuals to bring a publication to fruition, and *He Loves Me, He Loves Me Not* is no exception to the rule. For starters, I'd like to thank the fine folks at Adams Media for their support and encouragement. Innovation Director Paula Munier is a chick beyond compare. She's mom, mogul, intellectual, comedian, and sex goddess all rolled into one, and I adore her *way* more than chocolate. I'd also like to thank Editorial Director extraordinaire Laura Daly, copy chief Sheila Zwiebel, Brett Palana-Shanahan, Sue Beale, designer Colleen Cunningham, copyeditor Virginia Beck, and proofer Patricia Krumholz for their contributions to the project. A special shout goes out to Brendan O'Neill for his diligent work, professionalism, and exceptional humor, which, by the way, makes him a real catch (for any of you gals keeping score). Thanks, kiddo! And my humble thanks as well to publisher Gary Krebs for giving me the opportunity to offer up a few giggles to the female population.

Above all, I'd like to thank my friends and family, without whom nothing in life would be possible or amusing. Ma, Pop, Pookie, Glen, the Blonde Bombshell, Ellen and Jim, Jeans and Jim, Jim V., Karla, the Scribe Tribe, and especially Rick, whose unflinching support is the mainstay of my existence. I love and adore you all! I'd like to also give a special shout to Arjean Spaite, Ellen Weider, and Sarah Weider for their expertise, humor, and endurance throughout my research. And as always, thanks to Ma for all of her tireless work and support. And to those who shall remain nameless (you know who you are) I offer my highest regards for sharing with me your horrendous dating debaucheries. My condolences for all the tacky, tumultuous, adulterous, penny-pinching Neanderthals you've dated. I know your Mr. Perfect is right around the bend, so keep the faith! Thanks to you all.

Barb Karg

introduction

He loves me. He loves me not. Since the dawn of man, women have been asking themselves that question, and most of us are still searching for the answer. Does he really love me, or does he just like me? Is he playing me, or is he playing *with* me? Is he my soul mate, or is he just a heel? When I meet Mr. Right, how will I know?

Couples are brought together in any number of ways. In antiquity, cavemen simply dragged women to their dwellings by the hair. In the bucolic backwoods, farmers' daughters were traded for prize cows. Victorian women were married off for their dowries and inheritances. While today's stock and trade in the dating game has thankfully become more civilized, at times it's exceedingly more complex than in days of old.

As twenty-first-century women, we're faced with an enormous challenge when searching for a man, and when we finally find one, we have to spend a significant amount of time and energy deciding if he's Prince Charming or Prince Chump.

As a result, we modern gals are left no option but to play a dating game that requires tremendous skill, training, integrity, strategy, and an abundance of pure luck.

In order to find Mr. Right, you have to wade through a bounty of Mr. Tolerables and Mr. Wrongs and all measure of men who fall between those ranges. Finding the right man is a process not unlike that of going to the Humane Society in search of a compatible pet. Some puppies are so incredibly adorable that you fall in love instantly. Of course, they're usually not housebroken. Strays are a crapshoot. Some have potential; others have never had any social training. Older hounds are often stuck in their ways and are resistant to change. And forget the purebreds—they're all about appearances!

So how do you choose a guy? Like puppies, you have to pet and cuddle them. You have to see if they listen when you call them. Most importantly, you have to get a sense of their personality. Are they shy, stubborn, animated, outspoken, emotional, or serious? Is their bark worse than their bite, or will they nip at you from dusk till dawn? Finding the perfect loyal mate who'll never let you down is tough. But when you find the right mutt—you'll know.

Of course, selecting the right four-legged companion is much easier than finding the right fellow, but the principles are the same. This quiz is designed to give you an inkling as to whether or not your current or long-term partner truly loves you. Each chapter focuses on a specific set of questions, each representing aspects of your relationship with your guy, spiritual and emotional issues, and a variety of events, holidays, hobbies, life lessons, and family interactions.

It's my fondest wish that through this process, all of you gain a bit of valuable insight into your beloved gent and use what you glean to achieve positive results. Above all, I hope you have fun, have a few giggles, and ultimately find a bloke who fits you like a glove. No doubt, he would be lucky to have you! So pop open a bottle of your best cabernet, grab a box of Godiva, and take a ride on the wild side. Here's wishing you the best of luck in your pursuit of happiness, healthy living, a hunky stud to fill your days and nights with love and affection—and plenty of champagne and cashmere along the way. Cheers!

the dating game

The dating game. If only it could be as easy as the classic television show, where a single gal could ask a few pointed questions and take her pick of three handsome bachelors. But times have changed. Dating is no longer a question of "What's your favorite color?" It has now become an amalgam of queries and anthropological studies that closely examine a person's habits, psychological stability, emotional behavior, financial success, chemical compatibility, and rhetoric.

As women, we won't settle for the first guy who crosses our path. We take our time. We analyze. We scrutinize. We franchise. The dating world is more *Sleepless in Seattle* than *From Here to Eternity,* and that makes every encounter a test of social and spiritual compatibility. Luckily, some things never change, like the happiness or horror of a first date or kiss.

Dating is all about taking chances and careful study, and with luck, your man will pass the test with flying colors.

the first date

After months of chance encounters, the Calvin Kleinesque hunk you've been drooling over finally asks you out. First dates are always a big deal, and you're really excited. How does the evening go?

A. He insists you meet him for a seventy-nine cent coffee at Dunkin' Donuts.

B. You get all gussied up, but when getting into his car you find that his mother is in the front seat and will be joining you for dinner.

C. He takes you to a senior citizen's dance hall and says, "Isn't it great that they've got places like this for people like us?"

D. He invites you to a cozy sushi bar, pours your sake, and orders your meal in fluent Japanese.

E. He makes reservations at a five-star restaurant, picks you up on time, and insists you order lobster—because you deserve it.

ANSWER KEY: The First Date

A. Tar-like java at a doughnut shack is no way to start dating—no matter if he's a cop or not. **(1 POINT)**

B. He's Norman Bates. You may not live through the date. Grab the phone and warn your girlfriends! **(2 POINTS)**

C. It would appear your date has mistaken you for one of the Golden Girls. Direct him to the local senior center, and refocus your efforts on a man who is young at heart. **(3 POINTS)**

D. Anyone who knows how to properly order sushi is worth the effort. How will he do at a French restaurant? **(4 POINTS)**

E. Lobster? At market price? A second date is inevitable. **(5 POINTS)**

Score

kiss and **tell**

A great first kiss can send you soaring. A bad kiss can make or break a relationship. Kissing is all about compatibility and sheer animal magnetism. What was it like the first time your Valentino puckered up?

A. It felt like you were kissing a 200-pound red-spotted grouper.

B. He gave you a quick peck on the lips and asked, "What's for breakfast?"

C. He confessed that he hasn't had much experience, but he's a quick study who is more than willing to practice.

D. He offered up a short but sweet kiss that left you wanting more.

E. He kissed you long and slow and you felt it right down to the tips of your toes.

ANSWER KEY: Kiss and Tell

A. Kissing isn't about *Finding Nemo*. There are plenty of fish in the ocean. Toss this one back! **(1 POINT)**

B. A guy who thinks he's hit a homer before you've thrown your first pitch has already struck out. **(2 POINTS)**

C. Kissing is an art, and not everyone's a Van Gogh. With proper training, however, he could eventually paint a masterpiece. **(3 POINTS)**

D. A great smooch is like a fabulous truffle: You savor the flavor and then start anticipating the next piece. If your guy's a Godiva, he'll be well worth the wait. **(4 POINTS)**

E. The kiss that lights your fire will have you simmering in no time. Stoke up the flames of passion and bask in the glow. **(5 POINTS)**

Score

you've got
male!

Internet dating can be a ride on the wild side. If you're lucky it can lead you into the arms of Prince Charming. If you're not, you may find yourself in a pond full of frogs. You've recently met a great guy on the Internet and have had your first meeting. Prior to your date:

A. He indicated to you that he's had a few "minor" problems in the past. He then showed up for dinner with his parole officer in tow.

B. He told you he looks like Brad Pitt, but when you met at Starbucks he was short, tubby, and looked like Santa Claus.

C. He explained that he works in the film industry and turned out to be a checker at Blockbuster.

D. He described himself as an average Joe, but in reality he was the spitting image of George Clooney.

E. He made many claims about himself and he actually was who he claimed to be. You found him adorable and irresistible.

ANSWER KEY: You've Got Male!

A. Everyone deserves a second chance, but if your felonious fellow isn't allowed unsupervised visits, he's obviously got two strikes against him. Make bail before it's too late! **(1 POINT)**

B. What next? A sleigh bed and elves? Forget the mistletoe, honey. It's time to make a new list and check it twice. **(2 POINTS)**

C. Honesty is the best policy. You need to carefully entertain your options. This isn't necessarily as good as it gets. **(3 POINTS)**

D. Out of sight! Play your cards right and he could be yours from dusk till dawn. **(4 POINTS)**

E. Lucky you—you didn't get spam in your male box. Who says there isn't truth in advertising? **(5 POINTS)**

Score

dining out

Dining out is the consummate dating activity, and all of us ladies enjoy getting dolled up for a sumptuous meal with a handsome gent. Your fellow calls at the spur of the moment and asks you out to dinner. Where does he take you?

A. He drives through Burger King and orders three super-size meals for himself. For dessert, he's got a carton of Milk Duds in the glove box.

B. He takes you to the most expensive restaurant in town, but when the bill arrives, all five of his credit cards are declined.

C. He excitedly tells you about the corndogs down at the Zippy Mart—but you have to get there early while they're still hot.

D. He's partial to Italian, but he's willing to try that Vietnamese restaurant you've been hinting about.

E. He knows you love salmon, so he takes you to a great sea-food restaurant and has even reserved a table with a view of the sunset.

ANSWER KEY: Dining Out

A. If the best he can do is take you to see the King, he'll never treat you like a queen. This guy's a dud in more ways than one. **(1 POINT)**

B. Tacky alert! If you pay now, you'll be paying for the rest of your life. This man doesn't fit the bill. **(2 POINTS)**

C. You can't teach an old dog new tricks. See if he's willing to upgrade to Denny's for your next dinner date. **(3 POINTS)**

D. Your guy appears to have a cultural palate and the willingness to experiment. If you take turns choosing restaurants, you'll travel far and wide! **(4 POINTS)**

E. A thoughtful man like yours will leave you happy as a clam. Don't let the sun go down on this gracious suitor! **(5 POINTS)**

Score

SCORING FOR: The Dating Game

4 to 6 Points: Mr. Fishy All of us gals have had bad dates, but this guy flunked Dating 101. He's a cheap, blatant fraud, and locking lips with him is like kissing a blind carp. If you choose to go out a second time, shame on you!

7 to 11 Points: Mr. Assumption Dating, dining, and kissing are make-or-break events, and your fellow is making some bold assumptions. There's a slight chance he's trainable, but could you ever really forgive him for taking you to an AARP meeting?

12 to 16 Points: Mr. Conceivable Sounds like your potential beau is hit-and-miss. He could be a flop, but there is potential to pursue. The real question is, do you have the energy and patience to make him your main man?

17 to 20 Points: Mr. Scrumptious This boy's got game! He's open-minded and self-assured, mindful and tactful. And to top it off, his kisses send you swooning. If he's truly an Honest Abe, he could be your Mr. Right.

TOTAL SCORE FOR: The Dating Game

chapter 2

getting to know you

It's no secret that the dating world can be exhausting. Getting to *really* know a man is difficult, but it doesn't take long before you both begin to peel back the layers and reveal each others' true selves. We gals have certain individual criteria we use to concoct a pros-and-cons list to tell us if he's Mr. Right, Mr. Tolerable, or Mr. Wrong. Sometimes, the answer is blatantly clear. Other times, the water is a bit murkier. If a man goes pale when you mention commitment, is it because he's been burned so many times his brain has a fire exit or is it simply because he has the stomach flu?

Commitment is a serious talking point. It means accepting everything your man is and does, and that includes his mannerisms, his sociability, and how he inevitably copes with the bumps and potholes on the dating highway. Does your man meet the challenge with an open mind, or does he lack the skills necessary to maintain public and private decorum?

minding your manners

Common courtesy is a human requirement that's all too often overlooked. Everyone has good days and bad days, times when your mood goes south and your manners even further. Like any guy, your Mr. Suave has his moments, but are they few and far between or up close and personal?

A. He abuses the right of public and private flatulation with reckless abandon.

B. He can belch *Yankee Doodle Dandy* after only two gulps of his Budweiser, but he does excuse himself after the final chorus.

C. He knows how to set a formal table, complete with soup spoons, salad forks—and paper napkins.

D. He insists on opening the car door for you, but only on special occasions when you're dressed to the nines.

E. He believes common courtesy is paramount, whether he's talking to a CEO or a janitor.

ANSWER KEY: Minding Your Manners

A. No woman in her right mind wants to date a walking whoopee cushion. Grab your gas mask. It's time to clear the air. **(1 POINT)**

B. There's something to be said for patriotism, but burping your loyalty is perhaps not the best way to showcase it. Pass the Tums! **(2 POINTS)**

C. He may not live up to Martha Stewart standards, but he's well intentioned and ready for dinner! **(3 POINTS)**

D. Miss Manners would have a hissy fit, but as long as you're okay with it, that's all that matters. **(4 POINTS)**

E. A little class goes a long way. If he treats all others with equal respect then he's bound to make you proud. **(5 POINTS)**

Score

meeting
mom and dad

Introducing your man to your parents is a milestone in any relationship. One can never be certain how the meeting will go, but there's never a second chance to make a first impression—and your guy definitely made an impression.

A. His first words to your father were "Damn, your girl howls like a banshee, if you know what I mean."

B. For dinner with your parents he wore cutoffs, a John Deere baseball cap, and a T-shirt that said "I'm with Stupid."

C. He turned on the "charm" by listing every one of his own accomplishments since preschool.

D. He was so nervous that he called your dad "ma'am" and your mom "sir" for the first twenty minutes, but finally calmed down and redeemed himself by washing the dinner dishes.

E. With obvious sincerity, he told your folks he sees where you get your good looks and terrific personality, and he extolled your virtues all evening.

*Experts note that
men who are meet-
ing a woman's
parents for the first
time should follow
some basic tips.
Dress to impress,
be confident, make
good conversation,
be prepared for the
inevitable Q&A ses-
sion, and make cer-
tain you open the
car door for your
lady before driving
away—the folks will
be watching.*

ANSWER KEY: Meeting Mom and Dad

A. The evening didn't go well for Mr. Tactless, but he's healing nicely. The shiner Daddy gave him should disappear soon. Who's the screaming banshee now? **(1 POINT)**

B. It's dinner with the folks—not a tractor pull. Even the most hardcore redneck has a snazzy pair of Levis and boots. Careful what you do with this cowpoke! **(2 POINTS)**

C. Great-grandma might have been impressed that he played tuba in the third grade, but no one needed to hear Egoman toot his horn all evening. **(3 POINTS)**

D. Meeting the folks for the first time can be nerve-wracking, and jitters are a common occurrence. The fact that he was working so hard to make a good first impression means he might just leave a lasting impression on you. **(4 POINTS)**

E. Flattery will get him everywhere as long as he's sincere. Your charmer knows how to work a crowd. Better still if your folks can't wait to see him again. **(5 POINTS)**

Score

getting to know you

kissing
and making
up

You've had your first fight, and you think the world has come to an end. You're sobbing to your girlfriends. You can't concentrate. And your colon is rebelling. How do you and your guy patch things up?

A. He calls and tells you that forgiveness is a virtue, and he's willing to accept your apology.

B. You call your mother for sympathy—and he calls her too.

C. When you get home from work, you find him on your doorstep waiting for you to arrive.

D. You argue, cry, kiss, and eventually end up in the sack for a night of make-up sex.

E. The fight was so stupid that neither of you can remember what it was about, so you both end up laughing about it.

ANSWER KEY: Kissing and Making Up

A. There's no winning with this loser. If he always has to be right then he's all wrong for you. **(1 POINT)**

B. Every couple needs a mediator, but trying to influence your mother is bad family values. Tell the crybaby to call his own mommy. **(2 POINTS)**

C. A smart man knows when to raise a white flag. He made the first move toward ending your feud, so give peace a chance! **(3 POINTS)**

D. Not all arguments end on a high note, but when all is said and done if you're both singing the same tune, you're bound to make beautiful music together. **(4 POINTS)**

E. Laughter is the best medicine, and if you can see the humor in your disagreements it's likely you'll get through just about anything. **(5 POINTS)**

Score

being
committed

For most people, the difference between dating and officially being a "couple" is the sanctity of commitment. The concept of committing to another person depends largely on interpretation, and on that issue men and women can often differ. Like most men, your fellow is firm in his convictions:

A. He loves being committed to women. Many of them. All at the same time.

B. His idea of commitment is season tickets to the 49ers.

C. He equates commitment with custody and proposes seeing you twice a week and every other weekend.

D. He knows that you're the woman for him and he's ready to commit when you are.

E. Slow and steady wins the race is his mantra. When you're both ready you'll know it.

American couples don't waste much time getting to the altar, with the average engagement lasting just six months. According to the Guinness Book of World Records, the longest recorded engagement was sixty-seven years, with the happy couple finally tying the knot when they were both eighty-two.

ANSWER KEY: Being Committed

A. You should never be a pawn in anyone's dating game. If he can't commit it's time to quit. Tell him the match is over. **(1 POINT)**

B. It's safe to assume you know where his true devotions lie, but if he's more concerned with third down, it's time for you to scramble. **(2 POINTS)**

C. If the idea of visitation rights works for you, that's fine. But scheduling a relationship doesn't leave much room for spontaneity. Do you really want to settle for a part-time lover? **(3 POINTS)**

D. A wise man knows when to give you space and time. An impatient man keeps nagging at you to choose him or lose him. If he doesn't push, consider pulling him closer. **(4 POINTS)**

E. The epitome of commitment is making mutual decisions, and a guy who understands that concept can make the perfect companion. Man the torpedoes, full speed ahead! **(5 POINTS)**

Score

getting to know you

SCORING FOR: Getting to Know You

4 to 6 Points: Mr. Insufferable If the best you can do is this aloof whiner, there's trouble in paradise. Public outbursts and private ignorance prove he has absolutely no intention of getting to know the real you. Jump ship before he belches again!

7 to 11 Points: Mr. Megalomania This dude is confident—primarily in his ability to be incredibly daft and/or egomaniacal. On occasion, he shows a glimmer of potential, but it'll take a lot of training. Adopting a puppy might be easier for you.

12 to 16 Points: Mr. Imaginable Hanging out with this man can be a mental teeter-totter balancing between manipulation or emotional reciprocity. If he can commit, however, you may find there's more to him than is just below the surface. Dive in and see if still waters run deep.

17 to 20 Points: Mr. True Blue No man is perfect, but one who is genuinely polite, eager to solve squabbles, and exudes confidence should move to the top of your Male-Order list. There may be a few kinks to work out, but men like him are like a fine Bordeaux—they get better with age!

TOTAL SCORE FOR: Getting to Know You

love is in the air

Ooo la la! Does anything in the world smell as sweet as true love and romance? Let's face it—it's every woman's dream to find a knight in shining armor who'll whisk her away to another place and time. (And do so without spilling the champagne.) In reality, however, those knights are elusive little warriors. But every now and again there's a glimmer of hope, and we get lucky enough to find the love of our lives. If we're really lucky—he's got a car and a job.

Love and romance go hand in hand, but they're always strolling down a two-way street. And naturally there are crossroads and plenty of signs that can lead a couple to either the perfect destination or a hellish hideaway. As women, we are caring, nurturing souls who love unquestionably. Men do the same, but they generally prefer a more subtle approach. In the end, it's all in the planning, timing, and the amount of thought he gives to wooing and surprising you—with or without his armor.

that's amore!

Love is a many-splendored thing, or at least it should be. Proclaiming love for one another is an epic event—one that is pivotal to the success of any relationship. Is your Romeo truly in love, lust, or just killing time?

A. You told him you love him and he said, "How about those A's?"

B. He thinks love means never having to say *he's* sorry.

C. You mention the "L" word and he says: "Lesbian?"

D. He's never actually said "I love you," but he does say he adores you way more than his Lexus, and you take that as a good sign.

E. He's not sure about what life is going to throw at him, but he's certain about his love for you and he lets you know it every day.

ANSWER KEY: That's Amore!

A. Someone's not playing the love game! You're still a free agent. It's time to ship this shortstop back to the minors. **(1 POINT)**

B. Let there be no doubt in your mind that there's a bad ending to this love story. You deserve a man who worships you, not one who worries you. **(2 POINTS)**

C. He gets high marks for being in touch with his feminine side, but he's crossing the line between fantasy and reality. You may have to spell it out for him. **(3 POINTS)**

D. Never underestimate a man's love for his set of wheels. He may be going at his own speed, but if he truly loves you, he'll eventually park in lover's lane. **(4 POINTS)**

E. Life is full of uncertainties, but a guy who can pick the wheat from the chaff will lead you to a field of dreams. **(5 POINTS)**

Score

budding
romance

We love receiving flowers for any occasion—especially when there's no occasion at all. Roses, daisies, mums . . . it doesn't really matter as long as they're not dead and they arrive with a card. When it comes to all things floral, some men sneeze while others aim to please. How does your fellow rank on the botany meter?

A. He never gives you flowers. He feels it's environmentally reprehensible to pluck a daisy from its flowerbed.

B. He shows up with a handful of gladiolas he's heisted from the local cemetery and proudly tells you that he hates to see them go to waste.

C. He only sends flowers when he's apologizing for a wrongdoing—but they're always roses.

D. He often brings you handpicked wildflowers thoughtfully tied together with a satin ribbon.

E. He always sends gorgeous floral arrangements to your home and office—and delivers them himself.

ANSWER KEY: Budding Romance

A. This dolt is either cheap and clueless or running an underground floral antiterrorism organization. What a pansy! **(1 POINT)**

B. Recycling is admirable, but it's perhaps best to let this relationship rest in peace. **(2 POINTS)**

C. His heart may be in the right place, but the sight of a dozen red roses should never raise your blood pressure. **(3 POINTS)**

D. Romance is in the air. Obviously he knows his daisies from his dandelions. Jane Austen would be proud! **(4 POINTS)**

E. A man who has the courage to show his affection in front of your envious coworkers is the best of the bunch. Don't forget to tip the deliveryman! **(5 POINTS)**

Score

love is in the air

the perfect romantic day

What woman doesn't love romance? No matter who we are, we all have a little Jackie Collins in our blood, and you're no exception. It's a lovely spring day, and your man has invited you out. You've got Harlequin hopes, and he's got a plan. Where do you go?

A. He takes you rock climbing, then leaves you at the top of the mountain to fend for yourself.

B. He grabs a six-pack and takes you to the bowling alley.

C. He takes you for a scenic tour of the wine country but seems to be spending most of his time on his cell phone.

D. He prepares a lakeside picnic complete with caviar, pate, and cabernet, and even extra bread to feed the swans.

E. He rents the penthouse of a swanky hotel where you find champagne chilling, a plate of chocolate-covered strawberries, and a steamy bubble bath for two.

ANSWER KEY: The Perfect
Romantic Day

A. Did adventure boy actually think you'd
enjoy playing *Survivor*? Tell the cliffhanger
that you're cutting him loose. **(1 POINT)**

B. This guy is rolling romantic gutter balls before
you've changed your shoes. Let the alley
cat know he's over the foul line. **(2 POINTS)**

C. Everyone gets distracted, but when you're
on a romantic outing all bets are off. If he
won't go to voice mail—voice your opinions.
(3 POINTS)

D. Obviously he put some time and thought
into planning your sumptuous retreat, and
only an animal lover would remember the
swans. Nature boy is a class act! **(4 POINTS)**

E. What could be finer than a room with a
view? Pop the cork, order in, and soak up
the atmosphere with your high-style lover!
(5 POINTS)

Score

here's to you, mrs. robinson

Since the dawn of civilization men have been learning to seduce us with varying degrees of success. Some feel a chrysanthemum and a pack of Reese's Pieces will suffice, others prefer a bit of Dom and a box of Godiva. When the time is right, what's your dream guy's concept of seduction?

A. A twelve-pack of Old Milwaukee and a DVD of *Girls Gone Wild*.

B. A vibrating bed and a sack full of quarters.

C. Getting naked on a bear skin rug in front of a roaring fire, where he dozes off after the first glass of champagne.

D. A Saturday afternoon picnic where he hand-feeds you cabernet, pate, and chocolate-covered strawberries.

E. Whisking you away to a quaint bed and breakfast—in Tuscany.

love is in the air

Actress Demi Moore isn't the only woman who got it right when it comes to romancing a younger man. At the age of 103, Australian Minnie Munro became the world's oldest bride when she married her boy toy, Dudley Reid, on May 31, 1991. Dudley was a relative youngster at age eighty-three.

ANSWER KEY: Here's to You, Mrs. Robinson

A. The words "seduction" and "stag party" should never be used in the same sentence. Booze and bimbos are for frat-house Friday nights and *not* your boudoir. **(1 POINT)**

B. Mrs. Robinson is turning in her grave as we speak. **(2 POINTS)**

C. Obviously he knows how to set a mood. Next time slip a NoDoz into his Cold Duck. **(3 POINTS)**

D. Only queens are hand-fed. This man's got all the right moves! **(4 POINTS)**

E. Do not dump him under any circumstances—especially if he's got frequent flyer miles. **(5 POINTS)**

Score

love is in the air

4 to 6 Points: Mr. Embarrassment This fellow wouldn't know if Cupid shot him with an AK-47. His idea of romance is Jurassic, and his seduction practices wouldn't charm an aardvark. Love means never having to say you're sorry for dumping this guy.

7 to 11 Points: Mr. Aloof Your latent love bunny is definitely a work in progress, but it's doubtful he'll ever be your *piéce de resistance*. He does have moments of clarity, but if he's having trouble giving you attention now, he'll never give it to you later.

12 to 16 Points: Mr. Potential Your guy sometimes has trouble communicating his true thoughts, but he works hard to create the perfect scenario and is thrilled when you love it. If the pros outweigh the cons you could be in for a lovefest!

17 to 20 Points: Mr. Classy This gent instinctively knows how to show affection for his favorite lady. And he's no slacker in the seduction department, either. Looking for true love? He could be your knight in shining armor. If he rides up on a white stallion, saddle up and enjoy the ride.

TOTAL SCORE FOR: Love Is in the Air

chapter 4

in the mood

There's no business like show business, and when it comes to setting the stage for romance, there are plenty of props and scenery that can be used to create the perfect romantic encounter. Whether it's love in the afternoon or splendor in the grass, there's much to be said about how a man approaches romance and all the wonderful little things and nuances that go with it.

A man who can set a mood is worth his weight in honey dust. It could be as simple as stoking a fire or as lovely as whisking you away to a cabin in the woods. We love surprises. We love thoughtful gifts. And we love lingerie. Even the toughest tomboy has a satin teddy hiding somewhere in her bedroom! Men who recognize our likes and dislikes are ahead of the game. Men who can create an atmosphere that is lovingly luxurious will win high praise. Is your fellow a master of surprise or a villain in disguise?

the
boudoir

You can tell a lot about a man by his bedroom, and when it comes to romance, a man's surroundings are very important to us. We scrutinize his environment with eagle eyes and the tenacity of a five-star general. The first time you laid eyes on your man's bedroom, what did you see?

A. Handcuffs on the bedpost and a wall rack full of buggy whips and riding crops.

B. A round waterbed with pink satin sheets, wall-to-wall shag carpeting, and mirrored walls and ceilings.

C. His bed was made and appeared tidy, but there was a huge pile of laundry in the corner and his nightstands were dusty.

D. A tasteful but slightly overdone African-themed room. The zebra bedding was interesting, but the life-size carved lion's head was a bit intimidating.

E. A perfectly made king-size bed, chenille throw pillows with matching bedding, flowers on the nightstand, and votives on the dresser.

ANSWER KEY: The Boudoir

A. Apparently your chap feels that bondage makes the heart grow fonder. Buggy whips are an acquired taste. If they aren't yours, just say no! **(1 POINT)**

B. Crazy, baby! Your shagadelic stud is stuck in a time warp. Go-go boots were made for walking, so if you're not feeling retro, make tracks for the door. **(2 POINTS)**

C. He may pass off his unkempt room as the "maid's day off," but you've got to wonder when he last washed his sheets. See if he'll rise to the occasion when you give him a box of Tide. **(3 POINTS)**

D. At the very least you know he's a risk taker when it comes to design, but if there's a stuffed hyena on the bureau you might need to run for cover. **(4 POINTS)**

E. It's no mystery that we love our own beds, but you've gotta love a guy who keeps his room free of messy distractions. If he's got a plug-in air freshener, he's looking out for your best interests! **(5 POINTS)**

Score

in the mood

what lies **beneath**

Lacy underthings are every man's foible. Do they risk getting you something racy or go conservative? What if the size is too big or too small? Are edible undies part of the Atkins diet? What's your fellow's take on lingerie?

A. He thinks a camisole is an army tent, and if it can't be bought at Ace Hardware he won't buy it.

B. He gleefully proclaims that your brassieres are the same style his mother wears.

C. He doesn't try to make a parachute with the voluminous grandma underwear you occasionally wear.

D. He has Victoria's Secret bookmarked on his Web browser and insists lingerie be as much a turn-on for you as it is for him.

E. He vows that lingerie is secondary to his lust for you.

ANSWER KEY: What Lies Beneath

A. Sheet metal garters will surely chafe. His idea of "hard wear" is entirely delusional. Fix him up with your welder girlfriend. **(1 POINT)**

B. No man should be able to compare and contrast a woman's bra with those of his mother. Consider your Playtex options very carefully. **(2 POINTS)**

C. Real men can distinguish between fantasy and practicality. Keep him around if he can contain his giggles. **(3 POINTS)**

D. A man shopping online for lingerie just for you? If he ships overnight, you couldn't ask for more. **(4 POINTS)**

E. A smart man knows when to barter and when to garter. He's a keeper! **(5 POINTS)**

Score

all wrapped up

If there's one invaluable mainstay in any relationship, it's that we love receiving gifts from our steady beau. Guys don't always know what to get us, but a fellow who at least makes the effort is usually a cut above the rest. What kind of gifts does your sweetheart give you?

A. He rarely gives gifts, claiming he doesn't know what you like.

B. When he returned from a tropical vacation, he handed you a shirt that said, "My honey went to Tahiti and all I got was this lousy T-shirt."

C. Usually a lovely assortment of lingerie—four sizes too small. He bought them because they fit the salesgirl so perfectly.

D. A thank-you card from your favorite charity that shows he made a donation in your name.

E. A CD of romantic music for your iPod, accompanied by a hand-made card.

ANSWER KEY: All Wrapped Up

A. There's no good excuse for not giving something to the woman you love. Tell Mr. Cheap and Lazy that you're giving him the gift of freedom. **(1 POINT)**

B. How very charming. As a thank you, give him a T-shirt that says, "I just returned home from Tahiti and all I got from my girlfriend was a Dear John letter." **(2 POINTS)**

C. It's a rare breed of man who can correctly guess a woman's size. Perhaps next time he'll size you up before he sizes up the salesgirl. **(3 POINTS)**

D. The true spirit of giving is all about heart. Gifts are lovely to receive, but they're better if they're going to someone who truly needs them. **(4 POINTS)**

E. The best gifts in life are free, but a thoughtful gesture can last an eternity. If you're lucky, so will your fellow! **(5 POINTS)**

Score

in the mood

setting
the stage

Lovemaking and foreplay go hand in hand, and a man who can set the stage for a night of passion is icing on the cake. Every guy has ingredients for creating the prelude to a romantic lovefest, and your love bunny has a recipe all his own:

A. He feels that prolonging sex is unnecessary because he'll be finished soon anyway.

B. He thinks that Tantric yoga is a cranky character in *Star Wars*.

C. He vaguely understands the concept of foreplay, but often rushes through to get to the good part.

D. Occasionally he takes the time to set the mood, but only when *he's* in the mood.

E. He gives you long slow kisses from top to bottom and back again, and you're more than happy to reciprocate in kind.

ANSWER KEY: Setting the Stage

A. This isn't the Indy 500, and you're no pitstop. Obviously, you won't be crossing the finish line together. It's time to ditch the speed demon and find a better mechanic. **(1 POINT)**

B. You'll never feel the force with a guy who lacks the willingness to explore new galaxies. It may be time to fly solo. **(2 POINTS)**

C. Why rush to dessert, when you can begin with cocktails? Gently remind him that you'd find a bit of doting far more appetizing than rushing through the main entrée. **(3 POINTS)**

D. Warming up before the big game doesn't have to be a chore, and a well-prepared man knows that a little effort goes a long way. Imagine the half-time show! **(4 POINTS)**

E. Once the wheels are in motion anything can happen, and there's nothing sexier than a man who pays as much attention to you as you do to him. **(5 POINTS)**

Score

SCORING FOR: In the Mood

4 to 6 Points: Mr. Clueless Brace yourself, baby: Your flipped out boy toy needs to reinvent himself. Your fellow's notion of intimacy is petting Rover. Do you really want a guy who hears "teddy" and thinks Roosevelt?

7 to 11 Points: Mr. La-Di-Dah If your comrade's good intentions run the gamut from cheap bongo drums to edible undies, you're going to be disappointed from here to eternity. Buyer beware!

12 to 16 Points: Mr. Determined Setting a proper mood for romance is something most men learn by doing, and your amorous adventurer is still fine-tuning his intimacy game. A little training from you will go a long way.

17 to 20 Points: Mr. Impassioned Your boudoir buddy has his act together, and you're no doubt enjoying the show. He genuinely seems to understand what makes you tick when it comes to giving intimate gifts both in and out of the bedroom. This Romeo will make your heart go pitter-patter.

TOTAL SCORE FOR: In the Mood

chapter 5

in the bedroom

When it's time to get up close and personal, nothing says intimacy better than a good old-fashioned roll in the hay. Lovemaking is one of nature's inevitabilities whether you're a grouse, a gorilla, a CEO, or a cocktail waitress. It's what mammals do, and in most cases they do it well—or try to, anyway.

Women love making love. And no matter who we are, we have a mental list of things that make our heart flutter or our mood sputter. Finding the right partner can be as frustrating as buying a used car. No matter how you approach your search for the perfect sex partner, you have to drive a lot of vehicles before you decide to park.

Playing the sex game requires a lot of strategy and tactical maneuvering. Learning to make love is an ongoing process for any couple, and more than likely your guy has a style that's uniquely his. The real question is whether or not he's your Mr. Hot or Mr. NOT.

safety
first

In this day and age, safe sex is of paramount importance to everyone—especially you. Birth control is always a touchy subject, but if you're with Mr. Right you can do no wrong. What's your fellow's approach to sexual safety?

A. He takes your dog to the park to play diaphragm Frisbee.

B. He would prefer you wear the sponge so that after lovemaking you can scrub the sheets.

C. He becomes a Trojan warrior when asked, but should you really have to ask?

D. He always has a condom on hand and isn't afraid to use it.

E. He initiates a discussion of birth control methods so you can both decide what's most comfortable.

ANSWER KEY: Safety First

A. Time to find Rover a new playmate. This guy belongs in the dog house. **(1 POINT)**

B. Unless you're acting out a fantasy wearing your French maid's outfit, there's trouble in paradise. Leave him your dry cleaner's business card on your way out the door. **(2 POINTS)**

C. Better safe than sorry. Tell your Trojan he-man there will be absolutely *no* horsing around without a saddle. **(3 POINTS)**

D. One in the hand is worth two in the bush. A well prepared man is sexy as hell. **(4 POINTS)**

E. It takes two to tango and you've got a terrific partner. Keep dancing! **(5 POINTS)**

Score

the big "o"

Orgasms are the quintessential peak of any intimate relationship, one that in the past was rarely discussed. But times have changed, and every aspect of a love dance is fair game. When it comes to the big "O" your guy has opinions:

A. Orgasm? Isn't that the art of Japanese paper folding?

B. You're no Meg Ryan, but you can—and do—fool him on a regular basis.

C. He caught you faking and insisted on a "getting to know you" lesson. You've never had to do it again.

D. Tit for tat is his rule, and he lives by it.

E. He's your sex slave.

ANSWER KEY: The Big "O"

A. If he won't do the time, he'll commit another crime. Get him a copy of *The Complete Illustrated Kama Sutra* and pray he reads it cover to cover. **(1 POINT)**

B. If a pastrami sandwich is more orgasmic than your man, it's time to frequent another deli. **(2 POINTS)**

C. Real men ask questions and they have fun getting answers—from top to bottom. **(3 POINTS)**

D. Turn around is fair play. Just don't kiss and tell—you'll make your girlfriends jealous! **(4 POINTS)**

E. In this instance, slavery is a good thing. Let him drool and reap the rewards. **(5 POINTS)**

Score

fantasy
island

Fantasies are a part of any healthy relationship. They give you the chance to be someone you've always wanted to be or play out a scene you could only dream of. How has your fellow responded to fantastic adventures?

A. You dressed up in a leather bustier and thigh-high go-go boots and he told you that you looked almost as hot as his high school football coach.

B. You came home one day to find that he'd installed a trapeze over your bed—as a surprise for you.

C. "Tell me yours and I'll tell you mine" is his creed, and for the most part he plays by the rules.

D. He takes great pleasure in fulfilling your fantasies—even if it means dressing up as a French mime.

E. He encourages mutual sharing of both yours and his fantasies, but insists fantasies are an enhancement—not a replacement—for the desire he feels for you.

ANSWER KEY: Fantasy Island

A. A man who compares you to a football coach needs to work on his game play. Time to punt! **(1 POINT)**

B. He may be a swinger, but it's only a matter of time before he takes too much for granted and brings home a circus midget. **(2 POINTS)**

C. Share and share alike is a healthy approach, but only if you're both willing to let your imaginations run wild. **(3 POINTS)**

D. Only a man who loves you would spend a night playing Marcel Marceau. Clever girl! Mimes are good with their hands. **(4 POINTS)**

E. Fantasies are icing on the cake and should never be distractions. As long as you're his main focus, the sky's the limit. **(5 POINTS)**

Score

SCORING FOR: In the Bedroom

4 to 6 Points: Mr. Dolt   Hang on, honey! It's gonna be a long and bumpy ride. When it comes to sex, your wannabe Valentino is more nightmare than dream lover. Do you really want to get up close and personal with a man who has the sexual manners of a caveman?

7 to 11 Points: Mr. Long Shot   Your Don Juan sometimes knows what to do in the sack, but he still doesn't know what you do and don't like. If you're a betting gal, cash in your chips and find a guy who's playing with a full deck.

12 to 16 Points: Mr. Resolute   It takes a big man to successfully conquer the little issues, so give him a wide berth and see if he travels the highway or if he takes the scenic tour. Either way you'll have a blast.

17 to 20 Points: Mr. Va-Va-Voom   Lucky lady! Your Adonis is on the ball when it comes to lovemaking and the *joie de vivre* of intimacy. He may have a few quirks, but he's ready, willing, and able to please you no matter the circumstances.

TOTAL SCORE FOR: In the Bedroom

chapter 6

inner circles

As women, we innately know that there's no getting around the simple fact that all boys love to be boys—especially when they're in packs. It's one of life's unwavering inevitabilities, and one that has to be dealt with carefully lest your gentleman decides your attitude toward his outings and his friends is unacceptable. By the same token, turnaround is fair play. How does he handle your going out with the gals? Does he throw a hissy every time you plan a girls' night out, or does he give you plenty of room to spread your wings?

There's no way to predict how you will handle your man's inner circle and how he will handle yours. You and your guy just need to jump into the lake headfirst and see if you'll sink or swim.

your friends

Your friends are the foundation of your social existence. Some you've known for years and others are recent acquaintances, but you enjoy their company no matter what you do. Like most men, your fellow has definite opinions about the people you hang out with:

A. On too many occasions he's wondered out loud what your friend Bambi looks like in a thong.

B. On a good day, he refers to your girlfriends as a "gaggle of gossipy geese," and he's not kidding.

C. Short of shopping for shoes at the mall, he genuinely seems to enjoy spending time with you in the company of your friends.

D. He doesn't mind that some of your closest friends are men and you believe his sincerity.

E. He has no problem telling your friends that you're the love of his life.

ANSWER KEY: Your Friends

A. If he's not focused—and delighted—on how *you* look in a thong, it's time to send him and his Fruit of the Looms packing. **(1 POINT)**

B. Failing to appreciate your flock of friends can cause friction. Any way you look at it, someone's goose is liable to be cooked. **(2 POINTS)**

C. He may never get gushy over a pair of discount Manolos, but what man does? Getting along well with your friends is a step in the right direction. **(3 POINTS)**

D. A man who is secure about your having male friends possesses two great qualities—self-confidence and trust in you. Way to go! **(4 POINTS)**

E. His forthright nature and willingness to openly share his feelings is endearing. Aren't your girlfriends jealous? **(5 POINTS)**

Score

his friends

It's a pipe dream to think that everybody will get along beautifully, especially when it comes to you and his friends. No matter whether they're happily hitched or swinging singles, there's always a glimmer of anxiety that either flares or fizzles depending on how your man plays his hand.

A. He can't understand why you refer to his buddies as "that rabid pack of Neanderthals."

B. They consistently call you "the wench." He thinks it's funny and does nothing to straighten them out.

C. He encourages you to get to know his buddies—especially his female friends.

D. His friends genuinely seem to enjoy your company and happily include you in many of their plans.

E. They think that you're the best thing that's ever happened to him, and they let both of you know it.

ANSWER KEY: His Friends

A. If his friends are still sporting loin cloths and carrying clubs, it may be time to take a big step up the evolutionary scale. **(1 POINT)**

B. A man who does nothing to defend your honor will never be honorable enough for you. Take careful stock of his class quotient. **(2 POINTS)**

C. Implicit trust is an essential part of a healthy relationship. Getting to know his friends will help alleviate relationship jitters. **(3 POINTS)**

D. Boxing matches may not always be your bag, but it's nice to know that you're welcome to join in the manly mayhem. **(4 POINTS)**

E. If your guy's friends have his best interests at heart then they're friends worth having. All the better that they recognize your sterling personality. **(5 POINTS)**

Score

boys'
night out

If there's one undeniable fact about men, it's that boys will be boys, and more often than not, they must act on the overwhelming urge to congregate and howl at the moon. This could mean anything from going to a ball game to drinking to hitting the clubs. What does your guy do for a boys' night out?

A. He asks you for twenty bucks in singles for a night at the strip club.

B. He shows up at your place at three a.m., sloppy drunk, and swearing he missed you all night long.

C. He invites the guys over to play poker, but he pops his head out of the basement every now and again to give you a kiss.

D. He goes out to a sports bar with his buddies but is home before midnight and is relatively sober.

E. A couple of times a week he goes to his bowling league or meets with his barbershop quartet.

ANSWER KEY: Boys' Night Out

A. What's next? Fifty bucks for a trip to the Bunny Ranch? If you're not enough for Mr. Hot-to-Trot, it's time to find a better stud. **(1 POINT)**

B. Having a juiced suitor pounding on your door in the wee hours is sure to give you many sleepless nights. No one needs that kind of midnight rambler. **(2 POINTS)**

C. This guy's playing with a full deck. As long as he keeps his boys' nights in check, he's worth the gamble. **(3 POINTS)**

D. Everyone needs to blow off a little steam. It takes a smart man to know when he's had enough. Let him sow his oats on occasion. **(4 POINTS)**

E. Every man needs time with his own kind. All the better if he can merge male bonding with his favorite pastimes. He's singing the right tune! **(5 POINTS)**

Score

girls gone wild

Men aren't the only ones who need time with their own. We girls just wanna have fun, whether it's a coffee klatch, happy hour, or a day at the mall. When you go for a night out with your best girlfriends, how does your guy react?

A. He slips a GPS unit into your purse so he can monitor your every move.

B. He calls you every twenty minutes to ask when you're coming home.

C. He says that if you're going to go whoop it up, he'll be out cutting loose with his own buddies.

D. He doesn't care what you do, but he asks that you give him a call when you get home so that he knows you arrived home safely.

E. He slips you fifty bucks for cab fare in case you need a ride home and can't reach him.

ANSWER KEY: Girls Gone Wild

A. Unless he thinks you're a Russian spy and he's playing *Mission Impossible,* your every move is your own business. Check your phone for bugs and get off his radar. **(1 POINT)**

B. Paranoia will destroy you. If he's that much of a pest, let him know. But if he persists, call the Orkin man. **(2 POINTS)**

C. If separate nights out are a mutual decision that's fine, as long as he's not just trying to get your goat. Having fun isn't a competitive sport. **(3 POINTS)**

D. Checking in after a wild night is always a smart plan. Asking you to call him upon arriving home isn't asking much. Keep him updated! **(4 POINTS)**

E. It's nice to know you've got a safety net and that your guy has all the bases covered. You're both better safe than sorry. **(5 POINTS)**

Score

SCORING FOR: Inner Circles

4 to 6 Points: Mr. Creepy You're an adult and you don't need to be wearing a homing device or justifying your friendships to anyone. Break free from this love chain and report this hoodlum to his parole officer.

7 to 11 Points: Mr. Perplexing Your paramour is a conundrum. He often snipes about your friends, but then encourages you to get to know his buddies while he gets to know yours. Take careful stock of this bipolar relationship; it could drive you stark raving mad.

12 to 16 Points: Mr. Sincerity He may occasionally go on a bender, but it takes a confident, open-minded man to meld his and your inner circles. If you give him an inch, he won't take a mile. You could go far as a team.

17 to 20 Points: Mr. Trustworthy Real men give you room to move. Your sweetie allows you to breathe. Toss your worries aside, because this fellow's got your back for all the right reasons!

TOTAL SCORE FOR: Inner Circles

all in the family

For most people, family is the tie that binds. No matter the size or functionality of family members, both men and women hope that the partner they choose will be loved and accepted by their nearest and dearest. In reality, however, you've got a better chance of winning the lottery.

Meeting your fellow's family and his meeting yours can be utterly nerve-wracking for everyone involved. What do you say? How do you act? Is is okay to wear fishnets?

Mixing your beau into the friends-and-family stew can get tricky. If you have the right ingredients, everyone will be satisfied. Mess up the recipe, and your respective clans could lose their appetite for both him *and* you.

Whether it's a family reunion or private party, your man will be under close scrutiny by you, your friends, and all family members. Will he make you proud or leave you making excuses for his questionable antics?

your family

Everyone has a family in one form or another, and yours is very important to you. When it comes to your nearest and dearest your guy isn't shy about expressing his opinion:

A. He refers to your clan as *The Addams Family*.

B. He thinks your family has too much influence on you and that you're too dependent on them.

C. He doesn't mind spending time with your family, but he isn't keen on the fact that many of your family members constantly show up unannounced.

D. He admires how dedicated your family members are to each other and is eager to be accepted by them.

E. He calls your folks "Mom" and "Dad," and feels like he's truly part of the family.

ANSWER KEY: Your Family

A. Almost everyone has an Uncle Fester or a Cousin Itt hanging from their family tree, but insulting your entire entourage will stunt this relationship. **(1 POINT)**

B. Most family members have influence on each other, especially if they're close-knit. Is he looking out for your best interests, or is he a control freak? **(2 POINTS)**

C. Setting boundaries is always a smart plan for any couple. If he's okay with your relations calling ahead then there won't be any unexpected surprises for either of you. **(3 POINTS)**

D. Integrating your gent into your family can sometimes prove challenging. Your fellow's eager beaver attitude is certain to keep up family relations, as long as he doesn't go overboard. **(4 POINTS)**

E. In a perfect world your guy can become an extension of your family. If they start referring to him as a son, he's obviously made a lasting impression on them and on you. **(5 POINTS)**

Score

his
family

Your fellow has invited you to his family reunion. You've never met any of his relations before and have no idea what to expect. You're nervous, but he's confident that you'll find the event an enlightening experience.

A. The first thing his grandmother does is ask if you're a good witch or a bad witch.

B. Both of his ex-wives are there because they still consider themselves part of the family.

C. You spend the evening smiling and nodding—everyone speaks Bulgarian.

D. Everyone goes out of their way to tell you what a good boy he is.

E. He proudly shows you off to everyone, and they instantly fall in love with you. You immediately feel like one of the family.

ANSWER KEY: His Family

A. Obviously you're not in Kansas anymore. If he also found it amusing when his mother announced how happy she was that you have childbearing hips, it's time to click your heels and wish your way home. **(1 POINT)**

B. It's a rare woman who doesn't take issue with being in a room with her man's ex-wife. If he didn't give you a head's up, give him a thumbs-down. **(2 POINTS)**

C. Cultural barriers can be overcome. Did he act as translator or leave everything to your own interpretation? **(3 POINTS)**

D. How lovely to be with a man who has built-in references. Hopefully in time, you'll find out what a good boy he *really* is. **(4 POINTS)**

E. It's one thing to love a man. It's another to love his family. If they're wild about you, he probably is too! **(5 POINTS)**

Score

mommy
dearest

Most men have a special place in their heart for their mothers. Some worship the ground they walk on. Others would rather that mommy keep to herself. All of us gals take note of our man's relationship with his mother, especially the way he treats her. How does your gent feel about his mom?

A. He goes to visit his mother three times daily—up in the locked attic.

B. He's sometimes critical of the way you do things, often telling you, "That's not how my mother does it."

C. When his bossy mother insists you're doing something wrong, he tells her to mind her own beeswax.

D. He's delighted that you and his mother have a lot in common and that you enjoy one another's company.

E. He treats his mother like a queen, but he lets you know unabashedly that you're the jewel in his crown.

MAMA'S BOYS

According to United States Census statistics compiled in 2002, the percentage of male adults who live with their parents is rising gradually. Currently, 55 percent of men aged eighteen to twenty-four live at "home," a 3 percent increase over forty years. For men aged twenty-five to thirty-four, a surprising 14 percent are still in the nest, up from 11 percent.

ANSWER KEY: Mommy Dearest

A. There's always a place for mom when she's off her rocker—it's called Bellevue. **(1 POINT)**

B. There's a fine line between helpful hinting and criticism. If he's not open-minded enough to accept your methods, send him back to Mommy dearest. **(2 POINTS)**

C. You'll love a man who loves his mother—but you'll love him more if he sets boundaries. More power to him! **(3 POINTS)**

D. You and his mother both love canasta and *Dancing with the Stars* . . . who knew? **(4 POINTS)**

E. It takes a wise man to recognize that there's room in his life for both his mother and his lady. If he treats his mother with love and affection, you can bet that he'll treat you with equal respect. He's a gem! **(5 POINTS)**

Score

the social scene

Couples spend a lot of time socializing together with friends and family. You're throwing a cocktail party so that all of your friends can mix and mingle. You've gone to great lengths to create a tropical theme complete with tiki bar and umbrella drinks. How does the party go?

A. His friends show up with a keg of beer and a stack of Super Bowl Highlight DVDs, and your guy helps them set it up.

B. He hangs out with his friends on one side of the room while you break your neck trying to mingle.

C. Everyone has a great time, but after the party he goes to bed and leaves you to clean up the mess.

D. You've agreed to share the hosting duties, but occasionally you have to remind him to help out.

E. He's the perfect host. He introduces everyone, makes sure they all have drinks and hors d'oeuvres, and helps tidy up after the soiree is over.

ANSWER KEY: The Social Scene

A. It's a cocktail party, not a frat party. If he refuses to ditch the toga mentality, send him back to the animal house. **(1 POINT)**

B. A guy who won't mix it up with your guests is worse than a party pooper. If he can't learn to mingle, take him off your guest list. **(2 POINTS)**

C. There's more to a party than mixing drinks and telling jokes, and tidying up is no laughing matter. Mr. Life-of-the-Party needs to clean up his act. **(3 POINTS)**

D. It's easy to lose track when you're having fun. As long as you don't need a cattle prod, you and your guy can party till the cows come home. **(4 POINTS)**

E. A host with the most will take care of guests and see a party through from beginning to end. Celebrate his good graces! **(5 POINTS)**

Score

SCORING FOR: All in the Family

4 to 6 Points: Mr. Whipped Sorry my dear—your mama's boy has serious issues, courtesy Mommy Dearest, who obviously failed to instill a host of social graces in her little darling. And he has the nerve to diss your family?

7 to 11 Points: Mr. Ignorant There's an inherent cluelessness in your fellow that will require potentially never-ending supervision. Be warned: His inconsiderate behavior toward your friends and family will probably wear you down.

12 to 16 Points: Mr. Equitable In general, your guy is fair and willing to meet you halfway when friends and family are involved. But he does occasionally lose patience without fully examining the circumstances.

17 to 20 Points: Mr. Congeniality Your fellow seems genuinely motivated to become part of your family and have you become part of his. Take heart in knowing that most of the time, your social butterfly will charm both you and your nearest and dearest.

TOTAL SCORE FOR: All in the Family

getting real

Developing and maintaining a strong relationship with anyone takes work. The job is made harder by the fact that most men aren't known for emotional indulgence. It's safe to say that the majority of them try their best to keep a stiff upper lip when it comes to their true feelings, especially those close to the heart.

A man who can express emotion while at the same time keeping it realistic and under control is a man worth having. How he communicates with you on an emotional level can be a make-or-break situation. None of us likes a game player any more than we enjoy a guy whose moods rise and fall faster than a cheap facelift. If you're dating Mr. Right, you need to take careful stock in the way he deals with his emotions and how considerate he is of your personal space.

who's *that* man?

Sooner or later in any relationship, jealousy rears its ugly head. Most men have definite opinions regarding jealousy, and your guy isn't afraid to let you know where he stands:

A. He saw you leaving a restaurant with another man and punched him out straight away—no matter that it turned out to be your brother.

B. He assumes you're having affairs with all of your male friends, coworkers, the postman, the butcher, the baker, the candlestick maker, and anyone else who crosses your path.

C. He has gotten jealous on a few occasions in the past, but he always keeps it in check.

D. He has no problem with your spending time alone with your male friends, but admits that weekend getaways with them might make him a little edgy.

E. He's secure in the knowledge that you're an attractive woman and that it's only natural that you turn heads wherever you go.

getting real

ANSWER KEY: Who's *That* Man?

A. The moral of the story is, ask before you slug. Sounds like this hothead needs a refresher course in anger management—preferably in a different country. **(1 POINT)**

B. A man who becomes accusatory every time another man looks at you will never give you a moment of peace. Give him a permanent time out! **(2 POINTS)**

C. Every woman appreciates a bit of competitive maneuvering, but a little goes a long way. Keep your friends close but keep your guy closer. **(3 POINTS)**

D. Being jealous is part of human nature. As long as he knows where you stand and he's comfortable with it, you're good to go. **(4 POINTS)**

E. Who wouldn't love a man who's peacock-proud to have you by his side? No need to smooth feathers with this gent. **(5 POINTS)**

Score

no cheating!

Men cheat. Women cheat. And in the long run it always ends up badly for someone, no matter how amicably one tries to solve the situation. Is your man true blue, or is he snowing you? According to him:

A. He cheated on all of his ex-girlfriends but claims none of them really seemed to mind.

B. He's too afraid to cheat on you because you've got a mean right hook.

C. He says that the lipstick you found on his collar belongs to his mother—and you believe him.

D. As a former Eagle Scout, cheating isn't in his vocabulary, but he had a friend whose wife strayed, so the friend had an affair. In that instance, he felt his friend's indiscretion was justifiable.

E. He'd rather die than cheat on you. There's no better woman in the world for him—and he knows it.

ANSWER KEY: No Cheating!

A. Wake up call! They're all "ex" girlfriends for a reason. Cut your losses and run, and don't ever look back. **(1 POINT)**

B. Well done. Don't give up those twice-weekly boxing classes in the event he strays. **(2 POINTS)**

C. Accidents do happen, but if it occurs with regularity, you might consider consulting a forensics professional. **(3 POINTS)**

D. Everyone is entitled to his or her opinion. It might behoove you to know what circumstances he considers "justifiable" and gauge if he's being honest with you. **(4 POINTS)**

E. It looks like you've got yourself a one-woman man, so cut him some slack the next time he starts drooling over Juliette Binoche. **(5 POINTS)**

Score

going with the flow

Everyone has good days and bad, but the way one reacts to those times is highly individualistic. There's no denying that we are arguably known to be the more emotional of the two sexes, but that rule isn't written in stone. Your manly Rock of Gibraltar has his moments:

A. He's so passive that a hungry chipmunk could mug him for his lunch money.

B. He's a drama queen, and if his life is lacking chaos, he'll create some in yours.

C. Life is a rollercoaster. Today he's as bouncy as Tigger. Tomorrow he's as somber as Eeyore. On a good day he's somewhere in between.

D. He appears calm, cool, and collected most of the time but has to work hard at not sweating the small stuff.

E. For the most part he stays on an even keel, through clear skies or stormy seas.

ANSWER KEY: Going with the Flow

A. No man should lose his nuts to Simon, Alvin, or Theodore. If your fellow has no fight in him, then it's unlikely he'll ever fight for you. **(1 POINT)**

B. Frankly, my dear, you've got a diva dilemma. A man who's clearly embracing his inner Scarlett O'Hara needs to be gone with the wind. Hitch up your bustle and find a better Rhett! **(2 POINTS)**

C. Jekyll and Hyde syndrome can be exciting, but more often than not it's deflating and just plain exhausting. If he can make strides toward releasing his inner Sybil, you'll stop living in a cuckoo's nest. **(3 POINTS)**

D. It's hard to keep calm when enduring life's challenges, but fighting back is half the battle. A guy who'll keep himself in check will likely keep your things in perspective. **(4 POINTS)**

E. Sounds like your fellow knows when to set sail and when to put ashore. However your journey turns out, it would appear you're in for a harmonious cruise. **(5 POINTS)**

Score

space
and time

Privacy is an
unspoken rule
between friends and
lovers, and no one
appreciates having
their secrets revealed
to the masses. The
man in your life has
his own approach to
discretion, whether
you like it or not:

A. He gives you plenty of alone
time—you only see him once a
month.

B. You've changed your e-mail
password a dozen times and he
still manages to hack into your
private correspondence.

C. For the most part he's the soul of
discretion, but on occasion he
accidentally blurts out your intimate details, and usually at the
most inappropriate times.

D. He has a strong sense of protocol and would never reveal anything you didn't want him to.

E. If you've had a hard day, he
draws you a bath, lights a few
candles, pours you a glass of
cabernet, and lets you soak in
peace.

Early English bath-tubs were fitted with a shelf across the middle to hold food and drinks. The tubs were designed so that two people could face each other and enjoy a soak while partaking of beverages and snacks. Queen Victoria frowned on such intimacy, and sadly, the tubs fell out of favor.

ANSWER KEY: Space and Time

A. It would appear that you'd have better luck getting an audience with the queen. Tell Prince Gone-a-Lot the slipper doesn't fit. **(1 POINT)**

B. Common courtesy dictates that some things remain private, and that includes Inter-net messages. Change your password to "schmuck," and send the nosy ninny a Dear John e-mail. **(2 POINTS)**

C. Everybody goofs now and again. Let him know how you feel and remind him— often—what's safe and what's sacred. **(3 POINTS)**

D. A smart man knows how and when to be discreet. Rest easy. Your secrets are safe with him! **(4 POINTS)**

E. Rejoice in a man who'll help wash your worries away. Any chance there's a foot massage in your future? **(5 POINTS)**

Score ⬭

getting real

SCORING FOR: Getting Real

4 to 6 Points: Mr. Drama Queen None of us gals wants a Jekyll and Hyde companion, but unfortunately, that's just what you've got. Do you really need that much drama?

7 to 11 Points: Mr. Inconsistent When he's on a roll, your guy can be a pill. When he's calm, he's civil. His concern for you often sounds sincere, but that doesn't mean you always buy it. If you can't trust—this guy's a bust.

12 to 16 Points: Mr. Adaptability Occasionally your Romeo beats issues to death in order to calm himself, and that can get irritating. Not to worry, though; he's a quick study, and you should never have to warn him twice.

17 to 20 Points: Mr. Integrity Honesty is the best policy, and your guy typically keeps lines of communication open. He also recognizes that you work equally hard at your relationship. You may have a few spats, but you'll probably never go to bed angry with this man.

TOTAL SCORE FOR: Getting Real

heart of the matter

In a relationship, sharing and generosity don't just apply to material things. In fact, they command higher attention and adulation if they have less to do with materialism and more to do with kindness of the heart. The issue of moral support encompasses both of those traits and is something men secretly hope for and most women rely on. A man who gives of himself freely and without expectation could arguably be hard to find. But if you know what you want and have an open heart, you're more likely to find your dream guy.

If a potential Mr. Right has all the right stuff when it comes to sharing and caring, he likely ranks high on our male dating scale. But can he make a spiritual connection? The soul mate is the quintessential apex of our climb up the mountain of eternal love. Does your guy truly understand your inner journey, or is he hiking down the bunny trail?

share and share alike

In a relationship, both people need to be able to share their thoughts, fears, and dreams without worrying about how their partner will respond. Most men are notorious for keeping quiet, especially if they're under the gun. Is your cowboy the strong silent type, or does he chatter more than a caffeinated parrot?

A. He's a dentist's worst nightmare. Just getting him to verbally express his thoughts is like pulling teeth.

B. He shares every minute detail with you, including the fact that his nose itches, he's got $14 in his wallet, his cat has gout, and he always loses sleep on Thursdays.

C. He's good about sharing his everyday thoughts with you, but he tends to clam up and talk to his close friends if something is really bothering him.

D. He'll share most everything with you, but touch his Captain Crunch and there will be hell to pay.

E. He shares everything, whether it's his peanut butter and jelly sandwich, the events of the day, or his dreams of becoming an astronaut.

ANSWER KEY: Share and Share Alike

A. No amount of Novocain is going to get Mr. Root Canal to flap his gums. Unless you want to spend your life talking to a brick wall, it's time to fill the communication cavity once and for all. **(1 POINT)**

B. Too much information! You don't need a play-by play of his trip to Der Wienerschnitzel drive-thru or his subsequent turmoil in the loo. Remind the chatterbox that sometimes silence is golden. **(2 POINTS)**

C. Being left out in the cold can make for chilly nights. Express your concern and see if he'll warm up to you. **(3 POINTS)**

D. Some things are sacred, and every man has his limits. Break out your granola and enjoy your breakfast, comfortable with the knowledge that a man and his cereal have an impenetrable bond. **(4 POINTS)**

E. A man with an open heart is certain to find his way into yours. If he's good about sharing, he'll no doubt be caring. Don't share him with anyone! **(5 POINTS)**

Score

give and take

Any individual who gives generously of themselves is a desirable partner on all accounts. Your fellow has a very specific attitude when it comes to generosity:

A. He never donates anything unless it's a tax write-off.

B. He claims to be a generous person, but in reality anything he does is ultimately for his own personal gain or status.

C. He's generous to a fault with his time, energy, and friends—so much so that you hardly see him.

D. He can't afford to be generous with his finances, but he's happy to donate time and muscle to helping family, friends, and his favorite charity.

E. He has a generous nature and does what he can for other people and causes, but he's careful not to overextend himself or his resources.

ANSWER KEY: Give and Take

A. A tight-fisted nature can choke the life out of love. Unless you're an emotional masochist, there'll be little in this relationship for you. **(1 POINT)**

B. Self-serving generosity is a transparent ruse. Be wary of any favors this guy does for you—they may come with a hefty price tag. **(2 POINTS)**

C. Immersing yourself in everything from Saving the Peruvian Pigeons to Young Hippies of America is admirable, but when will he have time for you? **(3 POINTS)**

D. Good will is the sign of an unselfish soul. A guy who'll pitch in during times of need will always be there when you need him. **(4 POINTS)**

E. A man who finds balance with his generous nature is sure to put you at the top of his priority list. Take part in his giving, and share the rewards together! **(5 POINTS)**

Score

soul searching

Over the years, the term *soul mate* has become a popular buzzword, and the concept of finding someone who's truly meant for you is now intrinsically linked to the dating world. What's your fellow's take on the soul mate search?

A. He thinks his soul mate is his left shoe.

B. He's certain he has found his soul mate—she lives two floors down.

C. When you explain that you feel he's your soul mate he says, "My ex felt like that, and I still don't really know what to make of it."

D. He seems to understand who you really are most of the time, but sometimes he doesn't have a clue.

E. When you broach the soul mate subject, he smiles and says: "I've thought you might be my destiny from the moment we met. Now, I'm certain of it."

ANSWER KEY: Soul Searching

A. If your bloke's more concerned with his Buster Browns than finding the perfect pairing, you've got a real heel on your hands. Walk away and leave him to his *sole* mate. **(1 POINT)**

B. How proud you must be to know that his obsessive viewing of *Sleepless in Seattle* finally paid off. Get yourself a gallon of Häagen Dazs and take up voodoo. **(2 POINTS)**

C. Obviously your karmic hero is lost in the Matrix. If he finds his way out, he's yours. If he doesn't, he's doomed to live his life in limbo. **(3 POINTS)**

D. Soul mates don't have to be psychic, merely intuitive. He may not get the little things, but if he is the spiritual yang to your yin he'll know what to do if the going gets rough. **(4 POINTS)**

E. If he's truly your other half, you'll know. If he recognizes it as well, your karmic journey is destined to transcend all obstacles. *Namaste!* **(5 POINTS)**

Score

moral support

You've had a really bad day at work with a coworker and you're very upset. In an effort to calm yourself you decide to call your guy and vent. How does he respond?

A. Moral support? How much will it cost me?

B. He comes across as the epitome of sympathy, until he launches into a monologue about how bad *his* day was and how much worse it was than yours.

C. He acknowledges how upset you are, but politely asks if he can call you back at halftime.

D. He's there for you 100 percent through thick and thin and is a good listener, but he begins offering too much advice.

E. Your pain is his pain. He drops what he's doing so that you can talk things through and figure out the best possible solution to your problem.

ANSWER KEY: Moral Support

A. The best things in life are free, and offering unconditional moral support to a loved one is at the top of the list. Your upset is non-negotiable, so tell your emotional cheap-skate to take a hike. **(1 POINT)**

B. Discussing a bad day should never be a competition. If he's not there to help you catch life's little curve balls, he'll never be a team player. **(2 POINTS)**

C. If football trumps a teary-eyed girlfriend, your sports nut needs some serious life coaching. See if he's willing to go the extra yard. **(3 POINTS)**

D. The art of moral support is knowing when to talk and when to listen. Just because the advice is free doesn't mean you have to take it. **(4 POINTS)**

E. Support is all about balance and sincerity. Sometimes you give more than you get. Sometimes you get more than you give. Your guy knows how to listen and learn!
(5 POINTS)

Score

SCORING FOR: Heart of the Matter

4 to 6 Points: Mr. Callous Your heartless wonder is a verbal, emotional, and financial skinflint, and his "me first" attitude will leave you spent. He's the soul mate from hell.

7 to 11 Points: Mr. Passive Aggressive Your guy may appear supportive, but when it comes to matters of the heart, he doesn't typically rise to the occasion. He might occasionally lend an ear, but in the end this zebra never changes its stripes.

12 to 16 Points: Mr. Endeavor At his core, your fellow is a very giving soul, but he sometimes spreads himself too thin. If you let him know how you feel, he'll likely take your concerns to heart.

17 to 20 Points: Mr. Passionate Look, listen, and learn is your man's mantra, and for the most part he sticks to it. What you give this guy, you'll get back in spades. Baby, he could well be your true soul mate!

TOTAL SCORE FOR: Heart of the Matter

chapter 10

the real world

In this fast-paced world of day planners, deadlines, lunch meetings, and martini mayhem, it's hard to find time for love. How can you meet the perfect man when work tends to consume your every waking moment? And how do you make sure you're his equal, and not just an appointment?

Your career is no more or less important than your man's career. Your pantyhose may sometimes run faster than you, but that doesn't mean your ambitions should take a backseat to another driver. Men often claim that they're interested in career women, but it's no secret that more often than not, they're intimidated by a woman who can run her own show—much less finance it.

The question to ask yourself is what kind of man are you really looking for, and when you find him, will you be satisfied with his work ethic, drive, and ability to provide for himself and others?

your career

Women are just as important as men in today's work force and you're no exception to the rule. You've tried to take advantage of the opportunities that have opened up for you, and as a result, your man is very vocal about your career.

A. He lets you know that your career is very important to him—he'd starve without you.

B. He thinks it's okay for a woman to work, but when she has children it's time to kill her career and stay at home.

C. He sometimes struggles with the fact that you earn more money than he does.

D. He always encourages you in your current profession while occasionally nudging you to do better.

E. He's proud of your success and is well aware of the hard work it took you to get where you are today.

While Internet dating services are claiming responsibility for a growing number of romantic connections that lead to the altar, many marriages are the result of more casual socializing. About 10,000 vows are exchanged every year as a result of couples getting to know one another during coffee breaks at the workplace.

ANSWER KEY: Your Career

A. This freeloader appreciates your paycheck more than he does you or your achievements. Do yourself a favor and find a more worthy charity. **(1 POINT)**

B. The barefoot and pregnant mentality went out with *The Flintstones*. Your caveman has clearly defined lines when it comes to breadwinning, and that makes him a loser on the evolutionary scale. **(2 POINTS)**

C. A guy who gauges his self-esteem by your paycheck may never be able to maintain his emotional balance. Wisely consider your investments in case you choose to withdraw. **(3 POINTS)**

D. Encouragement is fine, but a nag is a drag. As long as his intentions are pure, don't dismiss his advice. **(4 POINTS)**

E. A man who appreciates your work ethic and drive to succeed will always be proud of you no matter whether you paint by numbers or run a *Fortune* 500 company. Give that guy a raise! **(5 POINTS)**

Score

his career

Men are often defined by their professional choices and how they integrate their career into their personal life. Some men are traditional, while others embrace the advantages of working on the fast track of modernization. How dedicated is your twenty-first-century fellow?

A. He refuses to join the work force because it's in direct opposition to his hippie ideals. He believes the universe will provide everything he needs.

B. He takes his career very seriously and everything else—including you—requires an appointment.

C. He has never been unemployed, even if it meant taking menial jobs to get by.

D. He's worked hard to get where he is and is constantly looking for ways to move up the corporate ladder.

E. He is dedicated to his profession, but is equally dedicated to making sure it doesn't consume his life.

ANSWER KEY: His Career

A. Life is full of patchouli wishes and pipe dreams for this sixties throwback. How many men really make a living selling macramé plant hangers? Tell him to fit in or get off the pot. **(1 POINT)**

B. All work and no play makes Jack a dull boy. Chances are good that you'll never make his "to do" list, so tell his secretary you'll no longer be taking calls. **(2 POINTS)**

C. A solid work ethic is admirable no matter what his profession. He obviously knows how to survive, but the question is, for how long? **(3 POINTS)**

D. It's one thing to climb the corporate ladder, but it's quite another to do it without stepping on any toes. Hopefully they're not yours! **(4 POINTS)**

E. Finding a balance between personal and professional life is akin to finding Neverland. If you can both keep things real, there's no telling how high you can fly. **(5 POINTS)**

Score

the almighty buck

Money makes the world go 'round, but it's often a point of contention between couples. None of us appreciates a miser anymore than we want a guy who's in debt up to his eyeballs. Every man has financial habits. How does your guy deal with monetary issues?

A. He always spends his paycheck long before he gets it and is constantly "borrowing" from you.

B. He's so cheap that pennies fear him.

C. He's not afraid to suggest dinner at fine restaurants, while at the same time cheerfully suggesting you go Dutch.

D. Occasionally he drops a couple of bucks to the homeless guy in front of his office.

E. He always says "a penny saved is a penny earned," but he's generous when it comes to spending money on his family, friends, and you.

ANSWER KEY: The Almighty Buck

A. Interest-free "loans" should cool your interest in this spendthrift. Watch your wallet! **(1 POINT)**

B. Skinflints can be as tight with their affection as they are with their money. You're worth a lot more than that. **(2 POINTS)**

C. Are you friends or lovers? Splitting the tab is fine on occasion, but don't sacrifice being treated like a lady. **(3 POINTS)**

D. Philanthropy is endearing on any scale. He's making a smart investment in his karmic bank account. **(4 POINTS)**

E. A man who is well grounded financially can be worth his weight in gold. What a payoff! **(5 POINTS)**

Score

ambition
in the blood

Since the dawn of mankind, ambition has driven men and women to astounding heights and abysmal depths. Self-betterment is a desirable trait for all individuals, depending, of course, on how they go about achieving their goals. Over the years, your guy has developed a unique approach to getting what he wants:

A. He's learned every trick in the book for staying on unemployment.

B. He dreams of becoming a chef but feels he's not quite ready to go full-time at McDonald's.

C. He appreciates your ambitions, but if your personal success surpasses his, he'll have a slight meltdown. He might, however, work harder in the hopes of getting promoted.

D. He's perfectly happy in his middle-management position and going to the gym five times a week. Who needs more stress?

E. He's always searching for ways to better himself and his life, and you find that motivating.

ANSWER KEY: Ambition in the Blood

A. If this guy put as much effort into working as he does working the system, he'd be a CEO by now. There are no benefits here for you. **(1 POINT)**

B. It takes a driven man to move from Big Mac to beef bourguignon. If your Wolfgang Puck won't slice and dice, consider dining à la carte. **(2 POINTS)**

C. The breadwinner gene is firmly entrenched in the male psyche, but his ego shouldn't hold either of you back. He'll either dump you or trump you, but only time will tell if either of you can work it out with class or contempt. **(3 POINTS)**

D. A man who's content with his lot in life can share some of that contentment with you. If it ain't broke, don't fix it! **(4 POINTS)**

E. The best matches are made on an even playing field. If you both play fair and stay true to your hearts, you can accomplish anything you dream of doing. **(5 POINTS)**

Score

SCORING FOR: The Real World

4 to 6 Points: Mr. Lackadaisical Grab hold of your bootstraps, honey, because your Neolithic, penny-pinching, freeloading chump will quickly bleed you dry on all levels. Head for the hills before it's too late.

7 to 11 Points: Mr. Control Freak Your guy may seem like an attractive partner, but he walks a fine line. He wants to be the breadwinner, doesn't care to be promoted, and will rebel if your salary is higher than his.

12 to 16 Points: Mr. Ambitious Your faithful warrior's a hard worker who's usually generous, but he can sometimes send mixed messages. Fortunately, his ambition will override any meltdowns and ultimately motivate him and you to do better so both of you can benefit.

17 to 20 Points: Mr. Generosity We all have our insecurities, but your guy manages to abate most of his. Best of all, he's supportive of your career ambitions and would be happy being part of a dynamic duo!

TOTAL SCORE FOR: The Real World

chapter 11

that's life!

As young girls, we imagined the route to matrimony as a lovely promenade along an idyllic pathway. More often than not, our travels resemble more of a romp through a construction zone. Strolling down the aisle into the arms of your true love can be one of the most marvelous and momentous occasions of your life. But the things that your partner thinks and believes will affect virtually every aspect of your life together, and you'll want to make sure that you're both working from similar blueprints.

Although millions of us take similar steps, our journey is indeed our own, and we find that the groundwork simply doesn't exist until we create it. If the road to marriage is a work in progress, you'll want to grab your hard hat and take over the project. With luck, Mr. Right should pass all your inspections with flying colors.

engaging
circumstances

You're really excited because at long last your chivalrous knight has popped the question. Like most life-changing events, it was a monumental occasion that neither of you is ever going to forget.

A. He asked *his* parents for permission, but they haven't gotten back to him yet.

B. You accepted his proposal, but instead of introducing you as his fiancée, he refers to you as his financier.

C. He's asked you to marry him but suggests you wait a while to make sure things work out for both of you.

D. During a walk in the park he turned to you and said: "Oh, what the hell. Wanna get hitched?"

E. He took you out for a lovely meal, got down on bended knee, and in front of everyone told you that "you complete him."

ANSWER KEY: Engaging Circumstances

A. If your future depends on his getting mommy and daddy's blessing, you may not want to give him yours. **(1 POINT)**

B. Are you his partner or his personal banker? Better evaluate your interest rate and consider closing your account before he bleeds you dry. **(2 POINTS)**

C. Who says you can't have a long engagement? Just make sure it doesn't turn into decades. **(3 POINTS)**

D. It may not be the most romantic proposal, but as long as he's sincere, does it really matter? **(4 POINTS)**

E. He certainly has a flair for the dramatic. A fairy-tale wedding may be in your future! **(5 POINTS)**

Score

to wed or not to wed

One of the most stressful events any couple faces is planning a wedding. All the pomp and circumstance enveloped in a whirlwind of friends, family, flowers, and finances can be a nightmare. You and your fellow are preparing for the main event, even though you haven't officially set a date.

A. While choosing invitations, he confesses that the only concern he has about being married is whether or not he can be faithful.

B. Your folks are footing the bill for a guest list of 100. He hands you his own list of 200 and tells your folks to cough up the balance.

C. You'd like to have a Greek-themed wedding. He's insisting on Viva Las Vegas, complete with Elvis impersonators. So you decide to serve moussaka and have an officiate dressed like the King.

D. You decide to elope and get on with your lives. Your families are shocked but neither of you cares. You're in love and you're happy, and they'll learn to live with it.

E. Both of your families are chipping in with a budget that fits your dreams to a tee. There's even enough in reserve for you to have a romantic honeymoon.

ANSWER KEY: To Wed or Not to Wed

A. Red alert! If your alleged Mr. Right is already having adulterous concerns, you need to call the florist and cancel the chrysanthemums. No one needs a fickle fiancé. **(1 POINT)**

B. So the skinflint miser wants a free ride to his nuptials, does he? If he wants to play, he'll need to help pay. Tell him to put up or get shut out. **(2 POINTS)**

C. Weddings are all about compromise, and no one says you can't have a Big Fat Greek Elvis wedding. If you both rock, your blessings will roll! **(3 POINTS)**

D. Weddings are typically a family affair, but in the end you and your guy will have to make your future decisions together. Might as well start now. **(4 POINTS)**

E. Marriage is a merging of both of your families. If you're lucky enough that everyone gets along, you're destined for wedded bliss! **(5 POINTS)**

Score

irreconcilable differences

At one time or another during most of our dating careers, we've likely dated a divorced man. But, whether he's been hitched or not, it's always interesting to find out your man's opinion on the subject. When you ask his opinions on divorce, how does he respond?

A. The only reason for divorce is infidelity, and he doesn't plan on getting caught.

B. It's no big deal. People do it all the time. The secret is to get a better lawyer than she does.

C. He lost everything including the kitchen sink to his ex-wife. He's hesitant to ever marry again.

D. Divorce is the last and worst step in a relationship. If you've expended every bit of energy trying to keep a marriage alive, you do everything you can to make the split amicable.

E. Divorce isn't an option. You can always work through your differences no matter what they are.

ANSWER KEY: Irreconcilable Differences

A. When the cat's away the mouse will play, and this tomcat is better left out in the cold. **(1 POINT)**

B. A man who has already planned his legal defense will never bear witness to the joys of true partnership. Dismiss him before he serves up trouble. **(2 POINTS)**

C. It's apparent that your guy is still recovering from Ivana Trump syndrome, and only time will tell if he can make another leap of faith. Offer up all the kitchen appliances and see if he'll eventually snap out of it. **(3 POINTS)**

D. Only a realist knows when every avenue is blocked and his options are exhausted. Could he really keep a split amicable? Let's hope you never find out! **(4 POINTS)**

E. Sounds like your fellow is in it for the long haul. If he's true to his convictions, there's a good chance he'll be true to yours as well. **(5 POINTS)**

Score

the kiddy pool

In every relationship it's inevitable that the subject of having children will come up. For both men and women who want to become parents, or those who don't, this can be a make-or-break deal. How does your fellow feel about children?

A. He has multiple kids from several different relationships, but he has no clue where they are.

B. He definitely wants to reproduce. It would be criminal not to pass on his perfect genes.

C. He loves the idea of staying home and raising kids—he'll have more free time for golf.

D. He wants to start a family, but not until you've had ample time together as a couple.

E. He wants very much to bring a child into the world, but only when he's financially stable enough to give the child a proper start in life.

ANSWER KEY: The Kiddy Pool

A. There isn't a woman on the planet who can condone a deadbeat dad. If he has no interest in his progeny, he'll never be the father you want him to be. **(1 POINT)**

B. When a woman hears the term *perfect genes*, she thinks Calvin Klein. Your guy may think his DNA is flawless, but his ego certainly isn't. **(2 POINTS)**

C. Having a stay-at-home man may work for you, but if the number of dirty diapers exceeds his par, you may have to bend his putter. **(3 POINTS)**

D. It may sound selfish, but if he's dedicated to spending quality time with you first, it's likely he'll dedicate plenty of time to his children. Enjoy before you deploy! **(4 POINTS)**

E. A sensible man plans ahead, especially if he's determined to build a solid foundation. Your potential family will likely benefit from that groundwork and so will both of you. **(5 POINTS)**

Score

SCORING FOR: That's Life

4 to 6 Points: Mr. Sleaze A monogamous relationship isn't your guy's forte, and neither is parenthood. Time to face the fact that your alleged prince is more chump than charming. Give him the royal boot!

7 to 11 Points: Mr. Hesitation Your potential mate is on the fence. He may genuinely want to take the plunge, but he's hesitant to jump. And when it comes to kids, he could hinder more than he helps. Buyer beware!

12 to 16 Points: Mr. Optimistic Perspective is a prime motivator for your man. You tend to make most decisions together. Kids and divorce can make him nervous, but if you're truly his Ms. Right, that'll likely never be an issue.

17 to 20 Points: Mr. Realistic There's little doubt that your chivalrous knight wants to make you his fair lady till death do you part. His heart is in the right place, and it obviously belongs to you!

TOTAL SCORE FOR: That's Life

chapter 12

yin and yang

Here's the granddaddy of all coupledom questions: Are we compatible or aren't we?

Any individual who's drawn to another is very much aware of the attraction. For us gals, it can be the way he looks or smells or smiles. It can be how he treats others, or his philosophies, or how he lives his life. It can be a single thing or a combination of many things, but regardless of your guy's spiritual, emotional, or physical substance—it's important.

The yin and yang are opposing forces and should come as no surprise to you if you're searching or have found a man whom you think has qualities that meet your criteria. Male opinions and approaches to life can differ greatly from ours. If Adam and Eve had a kitchen, they'd no doubt be squabbling over dirty dishes. Take a closer look at your gent. You may be pleasantly surprised or shocked by his score in the match game.

your compatibility

Relationships are a constant balance of give and take, but the most successful are those where both individuals are compatible in regard to life, love, and the pursuit of happiness. It's not easy to find a man who complements you mind, body, and soul, but it is possible. How compatible are you and your fellow?

A. Aside from being carbon-based life forms, the only thing you have in common is WWE Wrestling.

B. You're climbing the corporate ladder. He's an unemployed hippie who still drives a VW Bus.

C. On many issues you agree to disagree, and that doesn't usually cause any friction.

D. You haven't got that much in common when it comes to mundane chores, but you both love waterskiing, *I Love Lucy* reruns, and eating crackers in bed.

E. When you're together, everything you share seems enhanced. The sky's a little bluer, the house is warmer, and your baths are bubblier.

ANSWER KEY: Your Compatibility

A. Watching a bunch of sweaty men in tights may be entertaining, but it's not a match made in heaven. Body slam the hulk and count him out. **(1 POINT)**

B. They say that opposites attract, but they can often create the worst kind of clashes. If your yin and yang don't mesh, forget the sixties and bring yourself up to date. **(2 POINTS)**

C. The rules of compatibility aren't steadfast. Nowhere is it written that you have to like all the same things, but it helps if you can find common ground. **(3 POINTS)**

D. If you had absolutely everything in common, you'd be clones. Chores are always a sticking point, but having fun is what keeps a relationship humming. Pass the Ritz and the remote! **(4 POINTS)**

E. No one can maintain Nirvana forever, but if you're both breathing easy when you're together life will be a breeze. **(5 POINTS)**

Score

vocal
dynamics

Couples will never agree on everything, but if you can talk about your issues openly, you can work through any problems. Most men leave jabbering to the female population, but that doesn't mean guys don't have plenty to say. Is your fellow quick on the draw or is he a man of few words?

A. He's the strong silent type—you haven't had a meaningful conversation with him since July.

B. Day after day, he's utterly fascinated with every one of his own opinions.

C. His patented response of "Anything you say, dear" is sometimes frustrating for you.

D. He believes that communication is the key to solving all problems, and he never goes to bed angry.

E. You say tomato, he says tomata, but in the end you both understand one another, and it doesn't matter to either of you if you choose to disagree.

ANSWER KEY: Vocal Dynamics

A. If you've had more heart-to-heart conversations with the cat than your man, it's time to act. Buy Fluffy a case of Fancy Feast, then inform Mr. Talkative that the Buddhist monk you're dating is well versed in philosophy as well as Schwarzenegger trivia. **(1 POINT)**

B. One-sided conversations don't count as communication. Gift him a tape recorder so he can forever enjoy hearing the sound of his own voice. **(2 POINTS)**

C. Feigning agreement can be insulting. Let him know how you feel and see if he'll change his tone. **(3 POINTS)**

D. Assuming he doesn't analyze everything in true shrink fashion, you're already ahead of the game. **(4 POINTS)**

E. Differences in opinion keep the world an interesting place. Finding and maintaining balance will surely keep the embers burning. Fire away! **(5 POINTS)**

Score

yin and yang

the common cold

It's the dead of winter and you're stuck at home with a nasty cold. You haven't got any soup or cold medicine and you can't fend for yourself. What does your Dr. McDreamy do when you call him for assistance?

A. He tells you to suck it up and quit being a big baby. Then he calls your mother and tells her to come over and take care of you.

B. He shows up wearing a HazMat suit and drops off a few cans of Campbell's soup and a box of tissues.

C. He offers to take you to the doctor—if you *really* need him to.

D. He stops by the pharmacy on his way home from work so he can restock your medicine cabinet. Then he makes you a nice pot of tea before heading out to a basketball game with his buddies.

E. He immediately comes over, stokes a fire, wraps a comforter around you, and then makes you chicken soup from scratch.

yin and yang

119

ANSWER KEY: The Common Cold

A. Obviously your guy is lacking the tender loving care gene. You'd be better off spending *all* of your time with your mother. **(1 POINT)**

B. You've got a cold, not the Ebola virus. Unless he works for the Centers for Disease Control, spending time with him would be a hazardous waste. **(2 POINTS)**

C. Everyone has priorities in life; perhaps it's time for Mr. Reliable to rethink his. **(3 POINTS)**

D. His heart is in the right place, but he would've scored more points if he'd stuck around. **(4 POINTS)**

E. A man who truly loves you cares for you in sickness and in health. You'll be breathing easy in no time! **(5 POINTS)**

Score

shacking UP

Many couples today take up residence together either as a precursor to marriage or simply because they want to. For most, this is a huge step up the dating ladder—one that can require some adjustment. What happened when you and your guy moved in together?

A. He quit his job, hasn't shaved, and has been sitting in front of the tube watching Judge Judy for the past six months.

B. His formerly neat habits have disappeared. You've been wading through dirty dishes and laundry for months.

C. He now cleans the bathroom religiously—every Christmas and Easter. But he does do the vacuuming.

D. You work hard to make all decisions together about how to decorate and how to do chores, but for the most part you're the taskmaster.

E. You agreed to split the chores and the bills, and he's holding up his end of the bargain.

yin and yang

121

A. To err is human, to forgive, divine. If he doesn't clean up his act in a hurry, you'll forever resent his complacency. **(1 POINT)**

B. Did he mistakenly assume the lease included a cleaning lady? Your new roommate needs a pick-me-up. Hand him a list of chores and see if he'll mop up his bad habits. **(2 POINTS)**

C. He may be bathroom challenged, but at least he knows how to Hoover. Show him how to dust and see if he'll pledge to keep it up. **(3 POINTS)**

D. If you're comfortable cracking the whip that's fine, but if your guy's on the ball he'll pick up the pace. **(4 POINTS)**

E. You can't get a much better deal than finding a partner who follows through with his promises. That's good housekeeping! **(5 POINTS)**

Score

yin and yang

SCORING FOR: Yin and Yang

4 to 6 Points: Mr. Incompatibility It's a widely held belief that opposites attract, but in this case, your man *du jour* is an opinionated schmuck. Face the music honey—you have more in common with a Himalayan yeti.

7 to 11 Points: Mr. Contentious You may think your sweetie is the cream in your coffee, but you might consider switching to decaf. Your allegedly harmonious hunk can put you on edge. Think twice before brewing another pot of Joe.

12 to 16 Points: Mr. Amenable He's an occasionally clueless night owl and you're an on-the-ball early bird. But if he's a good listener and receptive to change, there's a chance he'll meet you in the middle. Consider him a work in progress!

17 to 20 Points: Mr. Compatibility The key to being compatible is communication and appreciating your partner's eccentricities. No one is perfect, but your guy complements you. Hang on to this fellow, especially if he vacuums!

TOTAL SCORE FOR: Yin and Yang

fun with dick and jane

There's little doubt that the invention of various entertainment sources has given couples an entire universe of options to explore. What was once a stroll through the woods or reading aloud by candlelight has evolved into Blockbuster and pay-per-view. Finding a common interest with your paramour may be as easy as chatting about *film noir*, discussing the latest *New York Times* bestseller list, or bonding over the fact neither of you owns a television.

Entertainment is an industry we all respond to, no matter our preferences. So how do you approach this massive glut with your man? First, ascertain what he likes and doesn't like. Is he an action spy-thriller kind of guy or more of a historical-epic renaissance man? Second, get a feel for how dedicated he is to his entertainment particulars and if he's open to new mediums. Third, find out if he's so obsessed with his favorites that he thinks, lives, and breathes nothing else.

the silver **screen**

Watching films is a popular pastime for most people, despite the fact that the male and female genders don't always agree on what to watch. When choosing a movie, your best boy typically:

A. Serves you fava beans and a nice Chianti during a viewing of *The Silence of the Lambs*.

B. Refuses to watch subtitled movies because he can't do two things at the same time.

C. Shares a box of Kleenex with you during *The Bridges of Madison County*, and then tearfully suggests you watch it again.

D. Is perfectly willing to compromise and watch *Sense and Sensibility* and *Enchanted April* if you'll sit through *Kill Bill* and *The Texas Chainsaw Massacre*.

E. Strives to pick out films that you'll both enjoy, but is willing to see anything you suggest—even if it means watching you drool over Johnny Depp.

ANSWER KEY: The Silver Screen

A. His intent may have been to impress you with his culinary skills, but you might want to rethink a second date until after the lambs stop screaming. **(1 POINT)**

B. It doesn't take a rocket scientist to comprehend *Crouching Tiger, Hidden Dragon.* Time to say *sayonara* to he who can't multitask. **(2 POINTS)**

C. There's something to be said for a sensitive male, but if he watches it again without you it's time for therapy. **(3 POINTS)**

D. There's symmetry to the art of compromise if you can both keep the blub and the blood in perspective. If you can, your relationship just might become a blockbuster. **(4 POINTS)**

E. A guy whose masculinity remains intact while watching *Chocolat* is worth keeping on your A-list. **(5 POINTS)**

Score

the cable guy

Over the decades, watching television has become an intrinsic part of everyday existence, but it's not everyone's cup of tea. How does your guy feel about small screen entertainment?

A. He's morally opposed to the concept of television, smugly stating that it "rots your brain, and makes you stupid."

B. He runs from the room screaming "Why, Mommy, Why?" when you flip on the Lifetime Movie Network.

C. He loves the Western channel while you prefer Sci-Fi. To meet in the middle, you opt for Discovery.

D. He's accustomed to being the master and commander of the remote, but he's willing to share custody with you.

E. He enjoys watching the tube with you. You both have your favorite shows, and viewing them doesn't seem to create many conflicts.

ANSWER KEY: The Cable Guy

A. It would appear that a satellite is not in your imminent future. Tell Mr. Rot's-Your-Brain that you're switching dating channels. **(1 POINT)**

B. Try tuning to the Cartoon Network to see if it calms him down. If not, consider sending in your application to *The Bachelorette*. **(2 POINTS)**

C. Cheesy Westerns and bad sci-fi flicks cancel each other out. You're better off watching *Mythbusters* anyway. **(3 POINTS)**

D. A man and his remote are rarely parted. His friends are convinced he's fallen for you big time. You go, girl! **(4 POINTS)**

E. Zen and the art of television. When there's a will there's a way, and obviously you've found the right frequency. **(5 POINTS)**

Score

fun with dick and jane

making music

Music soothes the mortal soul, whether it's classical, oldies, hip hop, or jazz. Musical taste is as diverse as international cuisine. You and your man make beautiful music together in many ways, but when it comes to tunes:

A. His idea of setting the mood is getting naked and insisting you both act out the Village People's *YMCA*.

B. His iPod consists of nothing but *Abba's Greatest Hits*—both volumes.

C. He "accidentally" buries your Harry Connick Jr. CDs so that he can showcase his Marilyn Manson collection.

D. He's a little bit country. You're a little bit rock and roll. But both get equal airtime whenever you're together.

E. He makes a point of exploring your musical preferences and doesn't hesitate to play your favorite CD after you've had a hard day.

ANSWER KEY: Making Music

A. Different strokes for different folks, but Barry White would be a better choice. **(1 POINT)**

B. Any man obsessed with *Dancing Queen* needs to get his disco in check. Sign him up for music appreciation classes pronto! **(2 POINTS)**

C. "Accidents" happen, but common courtesy would dictate that he asks before hogging the shelf. After all, Harry's a lot prettier than Marilyn. **(3 POINTS)**

D. A thoughtful man understands the art of compromise and is willing to merge his Garth Brooks with your Springsteen without flinching. **(4 POINTS)**

E. Any guy who willingly listens to the *Must Love Dogs* soundtrack is worth his weight in platinum. **(5 POINTS)**

Score

a dark and **stormy** night

The written word is a mainstay of civilized life, but an individual's choice of reading genre is highly subjective. Your man is an avid reader who:

A. Has an abnormal obsession with *The National Enquirer* and the *Weekly World News*, and considers them first-class journalism.

B. Is more Dr. Seuss than Steinbeck.

C. Is into *Siddhartha,* and despite the fact that you enjoy Harlequin, he respects your books as much as you respect his.

D. On any given night he reads aloud to you, whether it's the local news or Robert Frost. And most of the time you enjoy it.

E. Has read everything on the *New York Times* bestseller list and is well versed in many genres.

ANSWER KEY: A Dark and Stormy Night

A. If he can't distinguish between Woodward and Bernstein and Hillary Clinton giving birth to alien babies, it's time for the UFOs to beam him up. **(1 POINT)**

B. Sounds like your guy is more influenced by the Grinch than literary masterpieces. See if he'll swap *Horton Hears a Who* for *Catcher in the Rye.* **(2 POINTS)**

C. Mutual literary admiration is never a bad thing. Perhaps there's a series of Zen romance novels you'd both enjoy? **(3 POINTS)**

D. Nobody needs to hear the latest golf scores out loud every evening, but who cares as long as you love the sound of his voice. **(4 POINTS)**

E. Nothing is sexier than a man who can decipher a *Da Vinci Code,* accommodate an *Accidental Tourist,* or chuckle over Dave Barry. No need to read and weep over this bookworm! **(5 POINTS)**

Score

SCORING FOR: Fun with Dick and Jane

4 to 6 Points: Mr. Get-a-Grip If your tastes extend to the silly or the avant-garde, then you may be perfectly happy with this opinionated, cannibalistic goofwad. But chances are that you're not.

7 to 11 Points: Mr. Dubious Old habits die hard. If he's set on watching *Star Wars* or reading *The Cat in the Hat,* he'll do it— over and over and over. When lucid, he'll appeal to your good graces, but he's sneaky. Watch your back!

12 to 16 Points: Mr. Conciliatory Your guy isn't shy about compromising. Mind you, he does attempt to pull one over on you now and again, but he usually gets busted.

17 to 20 Points: Mr. Accessible Thank your lucky stars—this guy's versed in everything from Shakespeare to Nora Jones to *Gilligan's Island.* Not only is your chap highly intuitive, he's also receptive to sharing your favorite media. This guy's got a happy ending!

TOTAL SCORE FOR: Fun with Dick and Jane

chapter 14

life's little pleasures

Men and women who are negotiating their way through the sometimes successful but often tenuous dating pool know the value of having a special activity—especially if it helps them find a partner who shares the same interests.

There are a number of enthusiast venues where your and your beau's paths could cross. Exercise, adventure sports, outdoor activities, Web surfing, board games, motorcycling, do-it-yourself projects, and the dog park are just a few of the endless possibilities.

So how do you know if you and your guy truly enjoy similar recreational activities? If you're into carpentry and he likes to paint, can you build something together? Does he like taking your dog for a walk on the beach? Can you keep the same pace while jogging? You'll never know until you try, and only then will you be able to judge if your gent has genuine interest or if he's just going through the motions.

the petting ZOO

Animal lovers are some of the most devoted humans on the planet, and when it comes to finding a mate they take Fluffy's opinions and input very seriously. More than a few couples have split up due to one or the other's animal companion. How does your sexy beast handle pets?

A. He thinks your pet bunny would be terrific in an Irish stew with a nice merlot.

B. The first time he walked into your house, the cat threw up.

C. He loves all animals. He has them mounted all over his walls.

D. He's got a teacup poodle. You've got a Great Dane. So you compromise and add a kitten to the mix.

E. He loves to take your dog to the park for an afternoon of Frisbee—and he even remembers the pooper scooper.

life's little pleasures

ANSWER KEY: The Petting Zoo

A. Sounds like your carnivore has a fatal attraction to your pride and joy. Best you send Elmer Fudd packing before Bugs becomes the main course. **(1 POINT)**

B. Animals are surprisingly good judges of character. Fluffy cast her vote in no uncertain terms. You might rethink yours. **(2 POINTS)**

C. That knock at your door is PETA calling. Your big-game hunter just lost his license to thrill. **(3 POINTS)**

D. The truth about cats and dogs is that they can all get along. If your guy shares litter box duty, it's a fresh step in the right direction. **(4 POINTS)**

E. If Rover likes having him over, you'll have a dog day afternoon. All the better that he has no qualms about sweeping for land mines. **(5 POINTS)**

Score

the handy **man**

Over the past decade, the concept of "do it yourself," or DIY, has become a popular buzzword, with many couples combining their talents and attempting everything from fixing the toilet to designing a love den. Is your handyman captivated by his own creations or paralyzed by tool envy?

A. He takes the term *do it yourself* quite literally—he tells you to do it.

B. He thinks faux painting refers to art forgers.

C. He erected a shrine to Bob Vila in his workshop, which is brimming with every gadget created since the dawn of man.

D. His entire home is filled with DIY projects and they're actually beautiful and functional.

E. Though he doesn't have much DIY experience he's eager to learn—especially if it's something you can do together.

life's little pleasures

137

ANSWER KEY: The Handy Man

A. Now may be the time to channel your inner *Toolbelt Diva* and tell Mr. Won't-Do-It-Myself that your idea of home improvement is gutting your relationship. **(1 POINT)**

B. Rag rolling isn't a felony. If you can't get him to sponge, stipple, stencil, or stripe, head over to Home Depot and find a fellow who knows his latex from his satin finish. **(2 POINTS)**

C. Does any man *really* need a 16-speed triple-bladed titanium band saw with a fully automated backup generator? If he spends more time coddling his hammers than cuddling you, consider swapping your handyman for a hands-on man. **(3 POINTS)**

D. A guy committed to completing a project is likely to share his finishing touches with you. Sounds like he has the right tools for a perfectly constructed relationship. **(4 POINTS)**

E. What could be more gratifying than sitting in a room you've designed together? Sit back, relax, and enjoy the fruits of your labor! **(5 POINTS)**

Score ⬭

pumping
iron

Exercise is one of the keys to healthy living and happy loving. Fitness is an individual decision, but it can play a role when it comes to couples finding one another attractive both in and out of their garments. Does your guy practice some form of exercise?

A. His idea of a workout is curling a twelve-ounce can of Budweiser.

B. He's a complete exercise nut who gets miffed if *you* don't work out seven days a week.

C. He's determined to go to the gym as often as he can so he can live long enough to keep up with you.

D. He suggests indoor or outdoor activities that you can both feasibly do and enjoy, like walking, dancing, or bicycling.

E. He insists that sex counts as exercise and asks you to play often and for long hours at a time.

ANSWER KEY: Pumping Iron

A. Let him belly on up to the bar while you sashay out the door. Bottoms up! **(1 POINT)**

B. Hanging out with Richard Simmons may be a gas, but no one should ever be forced into *Sweating to the Oldies.* **(2 POINTS)**

C. His heart's in the right place. Let's hope his cholesterol is, too! **(3 POINTS)**

D. What could be more romantic than a bicycle built for two or a sunset walk along the beach? Click your heels just right and there may be a cha-cha-cha lesson in your future. **(4 POINTS)**

E. Is there any better way to keep fit than a roll in the hay? Feel the burn, baby! **(5 POINTS)**

Score

life's little pleasures

hi-tech,
lo-tech

You're a twenty-first-century woman who appreciates the convenience and common sense of cell phones, e-mail, and iPods. What's your fellow's take on technology?

A. He thinks Yahoo is a chocolate drink, Google is still just a huge mathematical number, and a Web browser is an entomologist.

B. He's still suspicious of the ATM and firmly believes that it's only a matter of time before machines take over the world.

C. His idea of roughing it is going four hours without his cell phone, fully insulated self-warming mocha mug, and platinum nose-hair trimmer.

D. He's giddy about his brand new 72-inch high-definition plasma-screen television and has no clue how to operate the remote—but he's not afraid to ask you for help.

E. He thinks modern electronics are cool and perfectly sensible. He's the kind of guy who'd buy matching iPhones so you can learn to use them together.

ANSWER KEY: Hi-Tech, Lo-Tech

A. No doubt he also believes that a Macintosh grows on trees in Washington state. Are you dating a caveman? **(1 POINT)**

B. Obviously, you've hooked up with a techno-phobe. Bless his little Amish heart! **(2 POINTS)**

C. If his entire Christmas card list consists of Sharper Image employees, it's time to send him to tech-junkies anonymous. **(3 POINTS)**

D. Only a self-assured modern man is willing to admit defeat in the face of technology. Maybe there's a titillating Tivo in your future? **(4 POINTS)**

E. Technology can be an evil temptress, but it can be great if you're practical and you can have fun with it. Sounds like you're two peas in an iPod. **(5 POINTS)**

Score

SCORING FOR: Life's Little Pleasures

4 to 6 Points: Mr. Shiftless Better suck it up, honey, because gastropods have more energy and ambition than your beer-swilling technophobic couch potato—and it's highly unlikely that he'll ever change.

7 to 11 Points: Mr. Enigma Your companion is a bit of a mystery. He knows all about tools, but thinks silicone sealer is for leaky breast implants. And he'll pet Rover, but he's got Rudolph mounted on his wall. Think hard. Is he fun or frightening?

12 to 16 Points: Mr. Substantial So your DIY darling actually finishes the projects he starts? Lucky you! Of course that's the kind of guy he is—dedicated almost to the point of obsession. Fortunately, he's game for just about anything.

17 to 20 Points: Mr. Magnanimous This fellow is PETA approved. Thoughtful and dedicated, he is constantly searching for gadgets and activities you can share. And above all, he counts sex as exercise. Is he a dreamboat or what?

TOTAL SCORE FOR: Life's Little Pleasures

chapter 15

the holidays

Think New Year's Eve and Valentine's Day are torturous when single? Try sailing through a hurricane of family feasts, decadent decorating, and costumed galas while attached. Having a man in your life during the holidays can be a joyous occasion, but it can also lead to more than a few spats and unexpected revelations. You just never know until the Yuletide bells start jingling or Cupid starts twittering.

As with most things in life, holidays are half willingness and half compromise. If your fellow can meet you in the middle, you'll have a great time. If he can't, then holiday mayhem will likely ensue. So how do you ensure that you and your holiday hunk have successful celebrations? Discuss what you both usually do and what you'd like to do, and see how you can make it work. Love means never having to say you're sorry on a major holiday. True love means he'll get you cashmere.

decking the
halls

Christmas is coming and this year you're looking forward to spending time under the mistletoe with your favorite elf. When you approach him about his Yuletide plans, does he give you a wide elfin grin or a look of sheer unbridled terror?

A. Bah humbug. He feels that Christmas is a hideous amalgam of mass commercialism and hype. He wants nothing to do with it.

B. You go shopping with him to find presents for his friends and family, whom he lavishes with expensive gifts. All you get from him is a fruitcake and a potted poinsettia.

C. He adores Christmas and feverishly decorates, from the fully remote-controlled nativity scene on his front lawn to the blinking lights and tinsel on his houseplants. And he has it all done by September.

D. He'd love to see you on Christmas, but he can't until after three o'clock because he's volunteering at a local soup kitchen.

E. He doesn't care much about presents, as long as he spends the holiday with friends and family—and especially with you.

ANSWER KEY: Decking the Halls

A. Sounds like your Scrooge needs a change of heart. Ask him to give you a jingle once he has dealt with his demons. **(1 POINT)**

B. What's next, a lump of coal? Your jolly old elf is more naughty than nice. For shame! **(2 POINTS)**

C. There's something to be said for enthusiasm, but if he starts hiding Easter eggs in January he may need a holiday intervention. **(3 POINTS)**

D. You've got to love a man who spreads good cheer in its purest form. Grab a ladle and give him a hand! **(4 POINTS)**

E. The true spirit of Christmas is sharing time with all of your loved ones. Yours is a man who'll bring joy to your world. Don't forget the mistletoe! **(5 POINTS)**

Score

auld **angst** syne

New Year's Eve is a time for reflection and for celebration. It's also a time for new beginnings and renewal of commitments to yourself and your loved ones. Your fellow knows that holidays are important to you—especially New Years—and this year he actually made plans.

A. He told you his New Year's resolution is to find another girlfriend.

B. At the stroke of midnight he was New Year's toasted and spent the next few hours spouting his resolutions to the porcelain god.

C. Despite having an afternoon nap, the New Year eluded him. He hasn't been awake past eleven in over a decade.

D. He eschews crowded New Year's blowouts and throws an intimate gathering for his friends, family, and you.

E. At the stroke of midnight he kisses you and whispers in your ear that he can't wait to spend another year with you.

ANSWER KEY: Auld Angst Syne

A. May old acquaintance be forgot—and the sooner the better. Your holiday hunk is a colossal waste of time. **(1 POINT)**

B. When the ball drops, the last thing anyone should be doing is the Technicolor yawn. Pray that his first New Year's resolution is to swear off the Cold Duck. **(2 POINTS)**

C. It would appear that your Rip Van Winkle is New Year's impaired. If he's smart, he'll bring you breakfast in bed on New Year's morning. **(3 POINTS)**

D. There's no time like the present to let those closest to you know how much you care about them. Were you his first kiss of the night, or did he go for Mom? **(4 POINTS)**

E. He's a man with a plan and it's obvious that you're a big part of it. Raise a glass and toast to the dynamic duo! **(5 POINTS)**

Score

the cupid conundrum

Valentine's Day. A holiday dedicated entirely to love. It's every single woman's biggest nightmare. But is that also true for a woman involved in a relationship? It's your first V-Day with your Herculean he-man and you have no idea what to expect. The question is: What's *he* going to do about it?

A. Nothing. He's still scarred by a grade-school crush who refused his Valentine's card.

B. He shows up at your door with a box of ninety-nine-cent cherry cordials and scurries off to have dinner with his mother at the Ritz.

C. He gets huffy when your spam blocker deletes the lame e-card he thought was so clever, but he's pleased about the single red rose and "Be Mine" balloon he left on your doorstep.

D. He sends you two dozen red roses, a lacy teddy, and a card telling you he can't wait to see you in it.

E. He picks you up, blindfolds you, and drives you to a secluded beachside hideaway for the weekend. Once inside, you find a chilled bottle of Dom, a gourmet picnic basket, and your man wearing nothing but his best Pierce Brosnan grin.

*The flower business
doesn't hold a bou-
quet of posies to the
greeting card indus-
try when it comes
to sheer volume on
Valentine's Day.
According to the
Greeting Card Asso-
ciation, over 1 bil-
lion Valentine cards
are purchased
every year, making
it the second most
popular card-
giving holiday (next
to Christmas).*

ANSWER KEY: The Cupid Conundrum

A. Some childhood traumas will never heal. It could have been worse—he could've told you that he killed Cupid on his last hunting trip. **(1 POINT)**

B. Abominable. Get back to the five-and-dime, Jimmy Dean, and take those stale cherry bombs with you! **(2 POINTS)**

C. When it comes to Valentine's Day it's all in the delivery, and your cheap cherub gets credit for trying—but not hard enough. **(3 POINTS)**

D. A dozen roses would please any woman no matter what the holiday. Two dozen and a teddy will get you a full house. Play your cards right and everyone's a winner! **(4 POINTS)**

E. Pinch yourself girl, because if you're not dreaming, you've got a dream guy. Even the flying cherub is impressed! **(5 POINTS)**

Score

the witching
hour

It's All Hallow's Eve, your favorite holiday of the year. You and your gent have been invited to a huge Halloween ball and you want to find the perfect costume. What does your guy suggest?

A. He'll be the Lone Ranger. You'll be Silver.

B. He's the sun, and you'll be a planet that revolves around him.

C. You go as a dominatrix and he as your slave. You can lead him around all night by a leather leash and collar.

D. He goes as Adam and you go as Eve, because when you're together it's pure paradise.

E. He'll be Prince Charming and you go as Cinderella because you'll undoubtedly be the belle of the ball.

ANSWER KEY: The Witching Hour

A. Tonto is turning in his grave. No woman wants to start trotting when her man calls "Hi Ho Silver." Tell the masked man to stop horsing around. **(1 POINT)**

B. Mr. Sunshine is certainly showing his true light. Find another date before you go supernova. **(2 POINTS)**

C. At least if you've got him on a leash you'll know where he is all night. If he strays, remind him that you're packing a whip and you're not afraid to use it. **(3 POINTS)**

D. It can get chilly in the Garden of Eden. You might consider a bigger pair of fig leaves and strategically placed apples. **(4 POINTS)**

E. If the shoe fits, dance the night away. Your fairy godmother would definitely approve. **(5 POINTS)**

Score

4 to 6 Points: Mr. Pathetic Cupid is reaching for a grenade launcher as we speak, because your holiday hunk is a serious party pooper. Your best New Year's resolution is to can this curmudgeon.

7 to 11 Points: Mr. Hypocrisy Your flippant little elf is a holiday hypocrite. He's generous with others, but gives you cheap, cheesy gifts. He thinks he's a holiday god, but think twice—he may be the harbinger of holiday doom.

12 to 16 Points: Mr. Earnest Holidays are obviously important to your guy. He always thinks of you and usually hits the mark when selecting gifts, so it's easy to forgive him for the crock pot he gave you last Valentine's Day.

17 to 20 Points: Mr. Adorable Break out the champagne and celebrate your sweetie's exceptional holiday decorum. Santa adores him, and Cupid wants him for his poster child. Could you ask for a better holiday playmate?

TOTAL SCORE FOR: The Holidays

chapter 16

special occasions

Birthdays, graduations, weddings, the Super Bowl, going-away parties, job promotions—there are a myriad of special occasions that often take place throughout the year. And like the major holidays, many of these occasions require forethought, patience, cuisine planning, and usually gift giving, all of which can cause even the steadiest of pairings to go ballistic.

How does your fair gent do when it comes to remembering you on your birthday and your anniversary as a couple? As is often the case, he likely requires a reminder that can range from a quick mention of the date to a Louisville slugger to jog his memory. What about his attending a buddy's stag party?

Will your buck do the right thing, or will he cross the road no matter the consequences?

If your guy is smart, he'll put some thought behind his actions. If he's not, you'll have to give thought to taking a new direction.

happy
birthday
to you!

With few exceptions, birthdays are a special day in everyone's life. Some people are partial to low-key celebrations, while others prefer to party till the wee hours. You never know what to expect from your guy. What is he likely to do for the occasion?

A. He gives you a gift certificate for a complete makeover with a card that says: "Hope this helps."

B. He gives you a cheap faux crystal wall clock and a card proclaiming he's giving you the "gift of time."

C. He tells you he thought about buying you a gift he can't afford, but decided it was the thought that counted.

D. He invites your family and closest friends over for a surprise pizza party.

E. He takes you on a carriage ride through the park, followed by a dinner of Oysters Rockefeller and filet mignon, and then a night at your favorite hotel.

ANSWER KEY: Happy Birthday to You!

A. Who's the beauty and who's the beast? Tell Mr. Vanity that the only thing that needs to be made over is your decision to date him. **(1 POINT)**

B. How thoughtful. Now would be the time to take fifteen minutes to find a new man. Toss the timepiece in a lake, and tell him *his* time is up. **(2 POINTS)**

C. Gifts don't have to be expensive to be well received. A thoughtful man would forgo a passing fancy and find a way to show his appreciation and celebrate your big day. **(3 POINTS)**

D. It's always a pleasure to share special times with your loved ones no matter what the occasion. Pass the pepperoni! **(4 POINTS)**

E. Romantic birthdays make cherished memories. You'll look forward to counting candles with this chivalrous gentleman for many years to come. **(5 POINTS)**

Score

special occasions

^a year
to remember

A pivotal day has arrived. It's your first anniversary as a couple, and you can't wait to celebrate. This is, of course, the common reaction of women the world over. For most men, it's a day they typically forget and spend the rest of the day apologizing for. Your faithful fellow has a few surprises in store for you:

A. He sends you a stunning bouquet of calla lilies and tells you he's getting back together with his ex-boyfriend.

B. When you mention your anniversary he says, "Oh my God. Has it been that long?"

C. He completely forgets but takes you to an idyllic bed-and-breakfast to make up for his snafu.

D. He sends flowers to your office, cooks you a romantic dinner, then gives you a satin peek-a-boo robe and a pair of fishnets.

E. He pretends to forget, but when you arrive home all of your friends and family members are there for a surprise party he's arranged.

ANSWER KEY: A Year to Remember

A. Oh boy. What a waste of a perfectly good year. Grab your girlfriends and throw yourself a mind-blowing pity party. **(1 POINT)**

B. Time flies when you're having fun, but it sounds like your time together has been an eternity for Mr. Complacent. Toss his Timex out the window and show him that time really does fly. **(2 POINTS)**

C. Better late than never. If you're lucky he might remember next year. **(3 POINTS)**

D. Clearly romance is in the air, but it would have been better if he also bought a sexy thong for himself for *your* viewing pleasure. **(4 POINTS)**

E. Ye of little faith! How could you not adore a man who isn't afraid to tell the world how happy he is to be with you? **(5 POINTS)**

Score

always
the
bridesmaid . . .

Unless he's a wedding crasher, there are few men on the planet who can honestly say they love attending nuptials. You've been asked to serve as maid of honor at a friend's wedding and you're taking your fellow as your date. What does he do?

A. He has a little too much bubbly and hits on the best man.

B. He passes out cold at the ceremony, just out of sheer fright.

C. At the receiving line, he kisses and congratulates the bride, but offers condolences to the groom for his life sentence.

D. He agrees that the taffeta dress you're wearing is a pink poofy creampuff from hell—but you look beautiful in it.

E. He proudly stands by your side for the entire night and pretends to have fun even when he's forced to dance with the bride's eighty-year-old grabby grandma.

ANSWER KEY: Always the Bridesmaid . . .

A. This is one of those times when you better let the best man win. Now hurry off and catch the bouquet! **(1 POINT)**

B. You're attending nuptials, not an autopsy. A man who's faint of heart at the mere mention of the phrase "with this ring" will never be able to walk down the aisle. **(2 POINTS)**

C. Getting hitched doesn't mean pulling a stint at the state penitentiary. He may have been courteous to the bride, but when it comes to your future he's dead man walking. **(3 POINTS)**

D. A guy who can overlook the fact that you look like the dusty-rose–colored cousin of the Michelin Man is worth his weight in tulle. **(4 POINTS)**

E. Attending a wedding can be an exhausting affair, especially if you're in the wedding party. Cheers to your fellow—he truly is the best man! **(5 POINTS)**

Score

going stag

Your guy is going to a bachelor party for his best friend. You know his friend has a reputation for being wild and this raises a red flag. In an attempt to alleviate your fears, your guy explains the reason he's going:

A. Hey! It's free food, booze, and naked chicks!

B. They're going to a sushi bar and then to an opera he's been dying to see.

C. He can smuggle you in so you can witness the mayhem first hand.

D. He wants to make sure the groom doesn't do anything stupid.

E. Stag nights bore him to tears, so he's only going to dinner and then ducking out to come home to you.

The notorious stag party of old is losing favor as a pre-nuptial bachelor tradition. A growing number of bachelor parties are eschewing strippers and booze in order to plan weekend getaways featuring golf, sporting events, or casino gambling. The reason? Grooms are older, more mature, and increasingly financially secure.

ANSWER KEY: Going Stag

A. It's one thing to eat, drink, and be merry. It's quite another to eat, drink, and be indiscreet *with* Mary. Tell the stag you're hunting for a better buck. **(1 POINT)**

B. This is a pretty fishy song and dance. What are they doing for a nightcap, crocheting doilies? **(2 POINTS)**

C. Unless you're a zoologist, there's no need to study this type of deviant animal behavior. Let him loose for the night and assure the gorilla he'll be missed. **(3 POINTS)**

D. There's a lot to be said for the buddy system. Both you and the bride-to-be will breathe easier knowing your guy is on groom watch. **(4 POINTS)**

E. Not all bachelors are willing to endure a night of drunken buddies and hired bimbos. A guy with the wherewithal to bag on a bad scene is a true dear. **(5 POINTS)**

Score

SCORING FOR: Special Occasions

4 to 6 Points: Mr. Tactless If his unbearably cheap and insulting gifts haven't thrown you over the edge, then his *Girls Gone Wild* mentality will. Send this loser to Miss Manners Boot Camp and celebrate your independence.

7 to 11 Points: Mr. Erratic Your man certainly enjoys special occasions, but his methods aren't always conventional. He might surprise you with a birthday gift, but it'll probably be very late. If you're lucky he'll make up for his erroneous ways, but sticking with him could be a big mistake.

12 to 16 Points: Mr. Heartfelt While he has an occasional lapse of judgment—like the time he threw you a surprise birthday party at Denny's—his charm and sincere intentions make it easy to forgive and forget.

17 to 20 Points: Mr. Panache Are there *any* females among us who don't like to celebrate in grand style? Your gent puts the "special" in special occasion, and does it with a style and panache that's uniquely his. He's the real deal, baby!

TOTAL SCORE FOR: Special Occasions

keeping up appearances

It's positively naive to suggest that physical appearance doesn't play a part in male/female attraction. Whether it's a smile, a look, a smell, a pair of tight Levis, stilettos, or an Yves St. Laurent tie—there's always something that strikes a chord in the visual and olfactory senses.

We gals tend to be more fastidious about our appearance than men are. After all, we've been cursed with a Dante's *Inferno* of makeup, perfume, high heels, miniskirts, fishnets, tampons, all measure of creamy concoctions, and an endless array of bejeweled trinkets. Men, on the other hand, have a bar of soap and a razor.

When we check out a guy, we're analyzing his appearance with the critical eye of an equestrian judge and the romantic standards of Danielle Steel. Does he smell nice? Do his clothes look clean? Is that hair really his? *Never* underestimate the power of our scrutiny. We would notice a man's loose button or an errant eyelash during a Category Five hurricane.

personal
hygiene

Physical appearance and chemistry play a strong role in a couple's mutual attraction, and there's nothing sexier than a guy who looks good and smells even better. Is your man a firm believer in keeping up a healthy appearance?

A. He has had a mullet since 1988, and he still thinks it looks cool.

B. He religiously takes a shower every morning—Saturday morning.

C. He has more lotions and potions than you do, and he can't pass a mirror without blowing himself a kiss and proclaiming "You look fabulous."

D. He thinks a close shave is just missing a deer on the highway, but he always showers and tries not to recycle his dirty socks.

E. He's always well groomed and concerned with his appearance and wouldn't dream of offending your olfactory senses.

ANSWER KEY: Personal Hygiene

A. Take a deep breath, Missy. It's clear that Mullet Man isn't the catch of the day. The dating pool is vast. Cast your net and try again! **(1 POINT)**

B. Your guy may be consistent, but Friday-night dates will bring you to tears for all the wrong reasons. If he's unwilling to wash up, hang him out to dry. **(2 POINTS)**

C. It would appear your Aqua Velva man is a bit high maintenance. If he spends more time looking at himself in the mirror than he does at you, your Estée Lauder stash may be in mortal jeopardy. **(3 POINTS)**

D. A bit of Brad Pitt scruff never hurt anyone. And as long as his socks don't walk out the door by themselves, you could do worse. **(4 POINTS)**

E. No matter his age, shape, or size, a well-groomed man is a sexy beast! Success never smelled so sweet. **(5 POINTS)**

Score

keeping up appearances

his
attire

Every woman loves a well-dressed man who isn't afraid to show some style and individuality. A guy doesn't have to be a metrosexual to love clothes, but a man who takes the time to dress himself for any occasion is often irresistible. Your hunky clotheshorse has his own style savvy:

A. If his clothes don't come in a three-pack from Wal-Mart, he won't buy them.

B. His closet is brimming with Hawaiian shirts so bright they burn your retinas.

C. He has an armoire full of Armani, Calvin Klein, and Hugo Boss. Slumming it for this guy is going to Eddie Bauer.

D. He's a T-shirt-and-Levis kind of guy who has no style, but he adores all the clothes you get him whether they're Sears specials or designer duds.

E. He has a style all his own, loves expressing it, and isn't afraid to experiment with anything new or vintage.

ANSWER KEY: His Attire

A. There's safety in numbers, but classy threads don't usually come in multipacks. Try another tailor—preferably one who avoids blue-light specials. **(1 POINT)**

B. Variety is the name of the game. One or two hibiscus prints are fine, but leave the rest to Don Ho. Life isn't a twenty-four hour-a-day luau. **(2 POINTS)**

C. They say that clothes make the man, but in reality it's the man who makes the clothes. Don't let Yves St. Laurent cloud your judgment. **(3 POINTS)**

D. A guy who appreciates your good taste is bound to appreciate you in other ways. He's not just window dressing! **(4 POINTS)**

E. It takes a confident man to be able to express his inner self and unabashedly show it to the world. Without question he has good taste—after all, he chose you, didn't he? **(5 POINTS)**

Score

your attire

A best girlfriend can get away with telling you that your derriere looks enormous in skinny jeans, but no guy will live to tell the tale. Just for fun, you send your man shopping and tell him to buy you an outfit for a night on the town. What does he come back with?

A. Five-inch-high lipstick-red stilettos, a black sequined bra with matching thong, and a pair of minuscule Daisy Dukes.

B. White Keds, a pair of khaki Dockers, a baseball cap, grey Notre Dame sweatshirt, and a purse you can fit a small child into.

C. A pair of ripped Gap jeans, a Jimi Hendrix T-shirt, tan Uggs, and a belt whose buckle doubles as a bottle opener.

D. A pair of stonewashed Levis, a low-cut but tasteful turquoise babydoll, leather slides, a drop necklace with matching earrings, and a hand-woven batik purse.

E. Black low-slung Calvin Klein dress pants and matching blazer, a white silk tank, silver slingbacks, and a silver clutch.

*Borrowing jewelry is
a tradition with an
entertaining history.
The first borrowed
jewelry worn to the
Academy Awards
was in 1944, when
Jennifer Jones was
decked out in glitter
from famed jeweler
Harry Winston. Every
year, the event
becomes one of
the most highly
protected security
zones in the world.*

keeping up appearances

170

ANSWER KEY: Your Attire

A. It looks like somebody has a dream girl whose image is better left pinned up in the restroom of an auto-body shop. **(1 POINT)**

B. Unless you're married with children, the soccer-mom look isn't going to get you past Arby's. He gets points for comfort, but he needs a Manolo Blahnik intervention. **(2 POINTS)**

C. Thinking outside the box is never a bad thing, assuming the grunge look suits your style. But don't pop open your Miller Light in the middle of Sardi's. **(3 POINTS)**

D. Not bad. If he didn't buy the babydoll from the Courtney Love collection, you might have a budding personal stylist on your hands. The hippie accent is risky, but at least he was willing to take the chance. **(4 POINTS)**

E. Someone's been watching the Style Network. He's obviously got an eye for what looks good on you, and isn't deterred by price or knowing when to mix and match. Do him proud, and wear him well! **(5 POINTS)**

Score

putting your **best** foot forward

Shoes are arguably the most misunderstood accouterment we possess. We're compelled. Our guys are confused. Why are we so obsessed with footwear? No one knows. It's one of the great mysteries of the universe. What does your man think?

A. He loves your taste in shoes and wears them often.

B. He's very polite. When you say "Jimmy Choo," he says "*Gesundheit.*"

C. He's clueless as to why you need forty-eight pairs of black leather pumps, but he does love the stilettos you occasionally wear.

D. He fully supports your shoe fetish and doesn't have a problem with you wearing high heels—even if you're taller than he.

E. He doesn't care if you're wearing Reeboks or four-inch stilettos, as long as you're comfortable.

keeping up appearances

171

ANSWER KEY: Putting Your Best Foot Forward

A. If he's wearing your heels, you have to wonder if he's been dipping into your lingerie drawer. If your thongs are stretched out, it's time to grab your Dolce and Gabbana's and run for the hills. **(1 POINT)**

B. When he says, "You paid *how* much for those shoes?" you say, "But honey, you gave me your blessing." **(2 POINTS)**

C. Doesn't every well-dressed woman have forty-eight pairs of black leather pumps? **(3 POINTS)**

D. It takes a big man to admit when he's height challenged—especially if he doesn't need therapy for it. He's no heel! **(4 POINTS)**

E. Any man concerned with your podiatric health is worth his weight in corn pads. Your boots are made for walking alongside this gent. **(5 POINTS)**

Score

SCORING FOR: Keeping Up Appearances

4 to 6 Points: Mr. Mullet Only one man could ever pull off a mullet, and unfortunately, your tough guy is no McGyver. If "tacky" were a designer clothing line, he'd be wearing it. Call *Queer Eye for the Straight Guy* and pray for a miracle.

7 to 11 Points: Mr. Unpredictable Oh boy. Your partner has a classic case of split personality and he's hopelessly caught between kitch and couture. He's alternately George Clooney or Milton Berle. Which one would you date?

12 to 16 Points: Mr. Wannabe Style's a conundrum for your wannabe fashion icon. He adores Tommy Hilfiger, but he's just as comfortable in Sears dungarees. Keep him in check and you'll both be dressed for success!

17 to 20 Points: Mr. En Vogue Major style points for your clotheshorse! He knows what he likes and isn't afraid to take risks. He exudes confidence and is proud to have you by his side. (Even if you're towering over him in stilettos.) You're stylin'!

TOTAL SCORE FOR: Keeping Up Appearances

eat, drink, and be merry

What a couple considers entertainment is never consistent. Some love to dine out and others love to cook for themselves. Other-dynamic duos find that travel is their bag, while some prefer puttering around the domicile. No matter how you choose to eat, dine, or retreat, you'll have a better time partaking if you've got a partner who appreciates your tastes and interests.

Seeing how a chap eats and drinks is seeing how he lives— and it can tell you a lot. Is he a porterhouse and Bordeaux sophisticate, a protein powder fitness buff, or a Cheetos connoisseur? The same can be said for how he spends his vacations and down time. Does he stop the car at the county line, or throw caution to the wind with an extreme-sport world tour? A man who's right for you will feed your soul and travel well, no matter where you venture.

in the
kitchen

Cooking is an art made in heaven for some, but for others is a territory better left unexplored. A guy who knows how to barbecue is always an asset, but one who knows his béchamel from his hollandaise is worth his weight in stainless steel. Is your hungry man a chef *du jour* or is he Chef Boyardee?

A. Poultry the world over is still in mourning after his first attempt at Chicken Kiev.

B. His idea of cooking is calling the Chinese take-out down the street.

C. His chicken gumbo doubles as tile grout, but his mother taught him how to make a mean veal parmigiana.

D. He's addicted to the Food Network and is game to try any recipe that strikes his or your fancy.

E. He loves spending a rainy day cooking all your favorite comfort foods.

eat, drink, and be merry

175

ANSWER KEY: In the Kitchen

A. If your guy is on the Chickens of America Top Ten Most Wanted List, you're going to need more than a wing and a prayer. Fly away home before it's too late! **(1 POINT)**

B. Take-out cuisine is fine on occasion, but every now and again everyone needs a home-cooked meal. See if he'll swap his wontons for an occasional tuna casserole. **(2 POINTS)**

C. His technique may be hit and miss, but if he sticks to what he's good at you'll have more Hungarian goulash and less heartburn. **(3 POINTS)**

D. A man who can decipher his weights and measures is destined to whip up good eats. If he makes a fabulous crème bruleé, kick him up a notch! **(4 POINTS)**

E. Food may be a way to a man's heart, but no woman can resist a thoughtful chef—especially if there's a chocolate soufflé on the menu! **(5 POINTS)**

Score

food and libation

Sustenance is an essential part of life and dating life, whether it be bread and water or champagne and caviar. Your guy may have a sophisticated palate or a penchant for pork rinds, but either way his relationship with food and libation is uniquely his:

A. He's convinced that Dom Perignon is an Italian director and that Beluga is a Russian province.

B. His pantry doubles as a bomb shelter—it's fully stocked with SpaghettiOs, Cheez Whiz, Twinkies, and several hundred boxes of Chicken 'n a Biscuit.

C. He's a meat-and-potatoes guy who thinks no meal is complete without a mountain of rolls and a bucket of gravy.

D. He savors the nuances of Chateaubriand, but also appreciates the complexity of carnival food.

E. He's willing to try anything once and can't wait to taste your favorite Ethiopian recipe.

THE FOUNTAIN OF YOUTH

Chocolate alert! Medical research shows that eating chocolate in moderation can actually prolong your life by reducing bad cholesterol and the risk of blood clots. Moderation isn't clearly defined, although the average American nibbles up about ten pounds of chocolate a year. The average Swiss enjoys over twenty pounds.

ANSWER KEY: Food and Libation

A. Chances are good that he doesn't know his cabernet from his chardonnay or his couscous from his capers. If he's unwilling to expand his palate, you're doomed to live an Oscar Mayer existence. **(1 POINT)**

B. Some foods may survive a nuclear holocaust, but this relationship won't make it past the expiration date. Resistance is futile. **(2 POINTS)**

C. An old-fashioned carnivore is good for comfort but hell on your cholesterol. You might consider changing your dating diet to include all the major food groups. **(3 POINTS)**

D. It's hard to dispute the excellence of a perfectly crusted funnel cake, but it's more fun to extend culinary adventure into uncharted territory. **(4 POINTS)**

E. A guy who's unencumbered by his palate will likely be open to experimenting with many of life's little pleasures. *Bon appetit!* **(5 POINTS)**

Score

a great escape

Everyone needs a break from the daily grind. The choice of how to spend valuable vacation time is highly individual. Some prefer adventure; others enjoy inactivity. You and your guy are planning a vacation. In his perfect world, what would you be doing?

A. Prepping for a carefree week off by stocking up on frozen dinners, a crate of DVDs, and a keg of Budweiser.

B. Staying at a lakeside cabin in the mountains where he can jet-ski, fish, and hunt small animals.

C. Glacier camping. No phone, electricity, or room service. Just you and the polar bears.

D. Sitting somewhere tropical with plenty of white sandy beaches, umbrella drinks, and scantily clad babes.

E. Going to Guatemala and volunteering to help victims of a recent hurricane.

eat, drink, and be merry

ANSWER KEY: A Great Escape

A. There's nothing wrong with the occasional couch-potato break, but do you really want to spend a week eating Swanson's and watching a *Bloodsport* marathon? **(1 POINT)**

B. Midnight strolls along a lake and a cozy fire-lit cabin sounds romantic—assuming Grizzly Adams doesn't smother you in camouflage and hand you a crossbow. **(2 POINTS)**

C. Obviously your guy has been bitten by the adventure bug. It could be peaceful being surrounded by stunning vistas. You could also be part of the food chain. Are you willing to grin and bear it? **(3 POINTS)**

D. Warm breezes and wild waves make for sexy tropical nights. Just make sure *you're* his eye candy! **(4 POINTS)**

E. It takes an unselfish person to take a week of hard-earned vacation time and donate it to helping others. He's got heart and soul, and you couldn't ask for more. **(5 POINTS)**

Score

that's entertainment!

None of us gals want to spend all of our time and energy keeping someone entertained, so a man who doesn't pester us like an untrained puppy is a welcome partner. Is your fellow easily entertained, or does he require constant stimulation?

A. If you leave him alone for more than five minutes, he hunts you down and asks, "What are you doing?"

B. The moment he gets bored, he takes your microwave apart to see what makes it work.

C. He's easily amused. Give him a rubber band and a Q-tip and he'll keep busy for hours.

D. In his idle time he'll ask if you need anything done around the house. If you don't, he'll break out the WD-40 and lube all your door hinges.

E. He's never bored. He always finds something to do, whether it's a DIY project, reading a book, or surfing the Net.

ANSWER KEY: That's Entertainment!

A. If you get him in the car and he starts repeating "Are we there yet?" haul him off to the dating day-care center and secure yourself some peace of mind. **(1 POINT)**

B. Experimenting on helpless appliances is one way to keep busy, but it's only a matter of time before you find your transmission in the living room. **(2 POINTS)**

C. A guy with an active mind doesn't need many props. You'll probably never understand what makes your McGyver wannabe tick, but as long as he's happy, you'll be happy, too. **(3 POINTS)**

D. A guy who can channel boredom into constructive energy can be a constant source of wonder. Give him a toothbrush and have him tackle the tile grout. **(4 POINTS)**

E. A fellow with an active mind is seldom confronted with boredom. Fortunately, they're also seldom boring. Lucky you! **(5 POINTS)**

Score

eat, drink, and be merry

SCORING FOR: Eat, Drink, and Be Merry

4 to 6 Points: Mr. Twinkie Your Jelly Belly monger clearly lives a very sad existence. Rubberbands enthrall him. His taste in cuisine is more Taco Bell than Tavern on the Green. He's a Ho Ho horror. Run!

7 to 11 Points: Mr. Jeopardy Roll the dice on this one, baby. Your dude is definitely more meat and potatoes when it comes to cuisine, and without a doubt, he's easily amused.

12 to 16 Points: Mr. Relaxed In the kitchen, your fellow is open-minded and isn't deterred by trial-and-error cooking. And you don't have to expend much energy keeping him entertained—most of the time.

17 to 20 Points: Mr. Cultured Idle hands and a lack of culinary expertise aren't a problem for your man about town. Rest assured, when you say "Dom," he thinks Perignon and not DeLuise. You'll travel far and wide with this dapper gentleman!

TOTAL SCORE FOR: Eat, Drink, and Be Merry

chapter 19

house and home

A man's surroundings and habits are a road map of his personality. Cleaning, gardening, laundry, shopping—all of these seemingly mundane chores offer a glimpse into a day in the life of your man. In some cases, it may help you decide if that guy is right or wrong for you.

Does he know his knits from his permanent press? Does he own an iron or a set of pruning shears? Does he shop for groceries twice a week or twice annually? Whether or not he passes muster is entirely dependent on what you consider acceptable. On the surface, you're grading him, but subconsciously you're wondering if you could live with him even if he's not spic and span.

In truth, there are very few who actually enjoy doing laundry, cleaning windows, and scrubbing toilets. And those who do are probably not men. So how does your guy rank on your household scale? Is he Mr. Clean, or will you have to clean up after him?

wash and wear

Laundry is one of life's necessary evils, and no one is immune. Wash, rinse, spin, dry. It's just like the dating cycle. Some things fade. Others retain their luster. Sometimes you need bleach to feel new again. "Men" and "laundry" aren't often heard in the same breath, but your guy has his routine in the bag:

A. His mother does his laundry for him three times a week.

B. He claims he doesn't understand the nuances of washing clothes despite the fact that you've been showing him how to do it for the last six months. He leaves so much laundry around that you usually end up doing it.

C. He takes great pride in his appearance. Everything is perfectly washed, ironed, and starched—right down to his sheets and underwear.

D. He washed his tighty-whities with his red sheets, but is secure in wearing his newly pink underwear.

E. He's been doing his own laundry for years. You'd trust him with your T-shirts and jeans—but draw the line when it comes to your fine washables.

ANSWER KEY: Wash and Wear

A. If mommy is still doing his wash, there may be a few diapers in the bag. He's not looking for a girlfriend; he's looking for a maid. **(1 POINT)**

B. There's a big difference between exploitation and ignorance. Take off the training wheels and inform the clueless wonder that you're tired of giving your All, and he's not worth taking a Whisk. **(2 POINTS)**

C. It's lovely that he owns a can of starch and knows how to use it, but he sounds a bit stiff. See if he'll loosen up. **(3 POINTS)**

D. Laundry is the art of washing like colors together. Maybe in time he'll come to understand the concept and learn to embrace his inner Clorox. **(4 POINTS)**

E. A fellow who takes laundry in stride is a load off your mind. Give him a smooch and a permanent press! **(5 POINTS)**

Score

to clean or not to clean

Like laundry, household chores are inescapable. No matter the size of one's personal space, there's always vacuuming to be done and dust to decimate. Many fellows don't own a can of Pledge, but that doesn't mean they aren't tidy. Your guy has a repertoire of cleaning techniques:

A. He hasn't cleaned his bathroom since the Carter administration and he named all of his cockroaches.

B. He seems to appreciate your own well-kept digs and suggests that perhaps you'd be interested in lending your housekeeping skills to his own. After all, his last girlfriend did it.

C. He's so anal about cleanliness that he catches your socks and neatly folds them before they even hit the floor.

D. He owns a toilet brush and he knows how to use it with vague regularity.

E. His surroundings are tidy without being obsessively immaculate, and he takes great pride when you applaud his efforts.

ANSWER KEY: To Clean or Not to Clean

A. If his home is a breeding ground for contagion, you certainly don't want to find out what's lurking between the sheets. Call the CDC before you catch something! **(1 POINT)**

B. Since when are girlfriends Merry Maids? Grab your broom and sweep this loser under the rug. **(2 POINTS)**

C. Nibbling crackers in bed is probably out of the question with this fellow. Unless you're equally obsessive, Mr. Uberclean will get on your nerves. **(3 POINTS)**

D. He may not be the best Tidy Bowl man, but he may improve with positive reinforcement. Don't flush him just yet. **(4 POINTS)**

E. Nobody's perfect, but as long as he's consistent and considerate you'll have more dates and less dust bunnies. **(5 POINTS)**

Score

house and home

188

how does his **garden** grow?

Maintaining a landscape can be yet another point of contention between couples. There is no yard god who will send one to hell if the weeds aren't whacked. A yard is more a measure of pride, willingness, and responsibility, and that's an individual decision. How does your lawnmower man feel about yard work?

A. He bought a sheep so he wouldn't have to mow his lawn.

B. He wanted a low-maintenance Zen garden. His front yard is a concrete pad with a single pot of fake flowers.

C. He keeps his garden relatively tidy, but he has an abnormal obsession with pink flamingos and garden gnomes.

D. He hires a gardener for the big stuff, but he handles the minor maintenance when he has the time.

E. He takes great pride in his landscaping. His yard looks like the cover of *Home and Garden*.

ANSWER KEY: How Does His Garden Grow?

A. Barnyard animals are a creative solution to yard work, but unless he lives on a farm, it's a *baaaad* way to keep up appearances. **(1 POINT)**

B. Wrong move, Grasshopper. There isn't anything restful about a concrete jungle. Nothing's coming up roses with this minimalist. **(2 POINTS)**

C. What next? Little forest creatures and Keebler elves? He gets points for effort, but see if he'll ditch the pesky micro-midgets for something more statuesque. **(3 POINTS)**

D. A man who knows his limits but still accepts responsibility will likely keep your relationship growing. Give him a green thumbs up! **(4 POINTS)**

E. Appearances count. If he takes as much care of you as he does his prize azaleas, your love is certain to bloom all year round. **(5 POINTS)**

Score

shop 'til you drop

Some of us shop to live. Others live to shop. It's no mystery that most of us fall into the latter category. If there's a sale, we will come—in droves. Men, on the other hand, shop only if they're starving or out of clean underwear. How does your guy do when it comes to shopping?

A. When he needs new clothes, he finds a new girlfriend to shop for him.

B. His idea of window-shopping is driving past the mall at sixty miles per hour.

C. He has a ten-minute rule. If he can't find what he needs in ten minutes, he decides he doesn't really need it and heads for the exit.

D. Shopping isn't his favorite pastime, but occasionally he accompanies you, and sometimes he even enjoys himself.

E. Even Steven. He'll go to the craft store with you and promises not to whine, if you'll go to the hardware store with him and swear not to start humming *I Will Survive*.

ANSWER KEY: Shop Till You Drop

A. Unless you're earning a salary as his personal assistant, introduce him to *www.walmart.com* and run off to warn your girlfriends. **(1 POINT)**

B. Obviously you're dealing with a mallphobic, and in truth, there really isn't a cure. You might be able to con him into getting across the threshold at Macy's, but he's sure to run from the store screaming if you head for the Chanel counter. **(2 POINTS)**

C. He's a man with a mission, and every minute counts. Pray he doesn't have a time limit on everything he does. **(3 POINTS)**

D. Amen and hallelujah! You've proven that any activity can be fun if he's with the right woman. Play nice and let him putter around Sharper Image. **(4 POINTS)**

E. A truly compatible shopping duo knows when to compromise. You may not always find what you're looking for, but you'll both end up feeling satisfied. **(5 POINTS)**

Score

SCORING FOR: House and Home

4 to 6 Points: Mr. Dirty Knickers Not only does your slob *du jour* refuse to clean, do laundry, and shop—he expects you to do it for him. Such repugnant behavior lands him at the top of Mr. Clean's hit list. Flush him out quick!

7 to 11 Points: Mr. Cut and Dry When it comes to cleaning, laundry, and yard work, it's all or nothing for your guy. He's Oscar or Felix, and either way there's no escaping his slovenly mess or anal retentiveness. Choose wisely.

12 to 16 Points: Mr. Rinse and Spin Overall, your chap is fairly consistent when it comes to household chores. And although he makes faces when you nag, he secretly enjoys having you around to keep him on the straight and narrow.

17 to 20 Points: Mr. Adept Your partner in grime has his cleaning act together. And when it comes to shopping, he's willing to compromise—especially if there's hardware store potential.

TOTAL SCORE FOR: House and Home

the material world

We all have items that we treasure, whether it's a favorite recliner, a cherished ring, or a vintage Corvette. Men and women all have a materialistic side, the difference being that some have the overwhelming need to acquire more stuff while others are content with a few choice things.

It's no secret that most men are into anything fast and furious that can do zero-to-sixty in the blink of an eye. It's also no mystery that we are typically guilty of having a soft spot for sparkly little baubles with high price tags.

Is yours a material boy who is all about toys, or is he happy with what he's got? If he buys you jewelry, is it from the heart or simply a show of status? The way your man deals with the material world is very closely tied to how he interprets art. When he gazes at a scenic mountainscape does he see the forest and the trees or does he see it only as a possession?

road warriors

Boys love their toys, and when it comes to toys, cars are often at the top of the list. There isn't a male on the planet who wouldn't give his right arm to spend three minutes zooming about in a Lamborghini. How does your Mad Max feel about his vehicle?

A. He drives a white windowless van filled with rope and duct tape.

B. He nurses a battered 1989 Hyundai with more mileage on it than a transcontinental jumbo jet, and yet becomes vague and elusive when you mention vehicle insurance.

C. He prefers a nondescript four-door sedan that he keeps in immaculate condition.

D. He loves his shiny new electric hybrid and feels that it's really a shame that more people aren't environmentally conscious.

E. He doesn't care what kind of car he drives as long as it's safe, well maintained, and you're in it with him.

Automobile registration records show that men tend to favor pickup trucks or luxurious high-performance cars with lots of horsepower. Women prefer cars that are affordable, practical, and safe. Generally speaking, men will often buy cars that appeal to women but it is a rarity for a woman to go for a "guy car."

ANSWER KEY: Road Warriors

A. Unless you and your guy are into bondage, it's safe to assume he's a serial killer. Drop what you're doing and dial 911. **(1 POINT)**

B. If you can't carry on a conversation over the sound of his muffler, it may be time to switch gears. You'll be in good hands with someone else. **(2 POINTS)**

C. A practical man enjoys function over form. He may not be fancy, but he's reliable, and he'll get you where you need to go. **(3 POINTS)**

D. If he's doing his part to take care of the environment, chances are he'll take good care of you. Less money spent on gas is more for the two of you to enjoy. **(4 POINTS)**

E. Who cares if it's a Porsche or a Plymouth? If he opens the door for you, hop in and enjoy the ride! **(5 POINTS)**

Score

the material world

learning from the masters

Art can be as varied as relationships and the men you have them with. One man's trash is another man's treasure, and that garbage and glitter is highly subjective. Is your art lover a Picasso man or a graffiti guy? Or does he even know the difference?

A. Prominently displayed in his living room is a framed poster of *Dogs Playing Poker*.

B. He thinks French impressionists are mimes.

C. He appreciates Monet, but he loves modern art. He can stare at a bull's-eye for hours.

D. He enjoys taking you to museums and gallery openings, but at the end of the day his favorite artist is still Gary Larson.

E. He's a Norman Rockwell fan, but he appreciates your eclectic Jackson Pollock obsession.

ANSWER KEY: Learning from the Masters

A. Have you ever met a woman who actually owns a print of *Dogs Playing Poker*? It's time to return to the Humane Society and find a better mutt. **(1 POINT)**

B. No doubt he's also convinced that Michelangelo is a quarterback for the Rams. Enroll him in an art appreciation course and see if it colors his imagination. **(2 POINTS)**

C. The fact that he can recognize a master artist is worth applause. The real question is whether he admires the simplicity of abstract art or is driven by an underlying compulsion to shoot Bambi. **(3 POINTS)**

D. There's no harm in living a *Far Side* existence. A guy who can grasp the eccentricities of the planet and its inhabitants is brimming with individuality. Take that, Red Baron! **(4 POINTS)**

E. An open-minded man generally possesses an open heart. Who says a relationship can't be both traditional and eclectic? **(5 POINTS)**

Score

home is where the hearth is

Men and women don't always agree on how to furnish and decorate their spaces. Men want simple comfort. We want elegance. In the end, we're usually embroiled in television and recliner warfare. No matter how your man fills his home, it's a reflection of his personality—and your guy has plenty of that.

A. His furniture consists solely of hand-me-downs, garage-sale finds, cinderblock bookcases, and stolen milk crates.

B. He doesn't know the difference between a duvet and a divan.

C. He has developed an interest in the Home and Garden channel. His first decorating attempt was faux painting a wall using pop-corn balls.

D. He loves all the furnishings you select but remains baffled as to why you feel his commemorative *Blue Lagoon* coffee table is an abomination.

E. He looks forward to the challenge of merging your modern Balinese style with his French colonial furniture.

ANSWER KEY: Home Is Where the Hearth Is

A. If there's a Donny Osmond bobble-head doll on the cinderblock bookshelf—*run!* **(1 POINT)**

B. He may think that a divan is a chicken dish, but if he's willing to learn he might have potential. **(2 POINTS)**

C. At least he's a risk taker. Try suggesting he paint with a brush or you're liable to end up with a bubble-wrap backsplash in your kitchen. **(3 POINTS)**

D. There's always room for compromise. Gently suggest he sell his pride and joy on eBay. Someone out in cyberland is bound to find a loin-clothed Christopher Atkins to be a conversation piece. **(4 POINTS)**

E. Sharing your personal styles will help you better understand and appreciate each other. Who cares if his Louis the XV chair is perched next to Buddha? **(5 POINTS)**

Score

diamonds are a girl's **best** friend

Every girl loves her baubles, whether they be costume jewelry or perfectly cut gems. Giving a ring to a special lady is a milestone in most men's lives. Your diamond in the rough wants to find you a ring. What do you think he'll give you?

A. A beautiful pear-shaped diamond ring that he originally gave to his ex-fiancée.

B. Anything he can find in the bargain bin at Walgreens.

C. A one-carat diamond that looks gorgeous but that he later confesses is actually a cubic zirconia.

D. A two-carat princess-cut platinum-set diamond ring—from Tiffany's.

E. A white gold emerald ring that he inherited from his grandmother.

ANSWER KEY: Diamonds Are a Girl's Best Friend

A. His recycling efforts may be valiant when it comes to newspaper and beer bottles, but recycling his previous fiancée's engagement ring as a symbol of his love for you is no better than dumpster diving. **(1 POINT)**

B. It's the thought that counts, but in this instance it doesn't count for much. Guys like him are a dime a dozen. You're worth more than that. **(2 POINTS)**

C. Nobody likes a counterfeiter, and he's made one whopper of a faux pas. He did admit to his stupidity, but if the ring is fake, what are his *real* feelings for you? **(3 POINTS)**

D. Good things come in small packages—especially if they're in a little blue box. Holly Golightly would be delighted with your good fortune! **(4 POINTS)**

E. Gifting you with a cherished heirloom is the height of devotion. Obviously, you've found your way into his family—and his heart. **(5 POINTS)**

Score

SCORING FOR: The Material World

4 to 6 Points: Mr. Atrocious Your material man has questionable artistic taste, college-dorm decor, and a serial killer van. If this is your dream guy—you need an intervention.

7 to 11 Points: Mr. Deception His wheels are practical and he's willing to give any decorating style a try. But no matter how much you like this dude and think there's potential, two words should seal the deal: cubic zirconia.

12 to 16 Points: Mr. Flexible Your refined gentleman knows what he likes and sticks to it. But that doesn't mean he understands why you don't like his glow-in-the-dark velvet Elvis. Patience, my dear, this too shall pass.

17 to 20 Points: Mr. Cosmopolitan Yowsa! Your material boy is ready, willing, and able to entice your creative mind, body, and soul. His cosmopolitan attitude extends to many aspects of his life, and that's both refreshing and irresistible.

TOTAL SCORE FOR: The Material World

scoring

Now it's time to commence with the scoring so you can find out if your beau loves you, likes you, or if he needs to be eliminated from the dating pool. Start by listing your score from each chapter, total all of your scores, and then check the descriptions that follow.

Chapter 1	The Dating Game	
Chapter 2	Getting to Know You	
Chapter 3	Love Is in the Air	
Chapter 4	In the Mood	
Chapter 5	In the Bedroom	
Chapter 6	Inner Circles	
Chapter 7	All in the Family	
Chapter 8	Getting Real	
Chapter 9	Heart of the Matter	
Chapter 10	The Real World	
Chapter 11	That's Life	
Chapter 12	Yin and Yang	
Chapter 13	Fun with Dick and Jane	
Chapter 14	Life's Little Pleasures	
Chapter 15	The Holidays	
Chapter 16	Special Occasions	
Chapter 17	Keeping Up Appearances	
Chapter 18	Eat, Drink, and Be Merry	
Chapter 19	House and Home	
Chapter 20	The Material World	
TOTAL:		

0 to 80 points: Mr. Wrong

Honey, if your knight in shining armor falls into this category, he's probably wearing flip flops, driving a Pinto, and is hitting on your little sister as we speak. Chances are that this will come as no surprise to you because men like him have little respect for women no matter their age, shape, personality, or status in life. Without a doubt, he's at the shallow end of the dating pool, and he has no intention of swimming upstream.

When it comes to daily living, Mr. Wrong expects a free ride. Having a steady career doesn't really concern him as long as he's got enough pocket change for pay-per-view, a twelve-pack, and a bucket of Kentucky Fried Chicken. On the home front, he's more Oscar than Felix. And be warned: He's not looking for a lifetime partner—he's looking for a cleaning lady.

In truth, this bad boy is as miserly with his emotions as he is with his wallet. He's not a caring and sharing man, instead favoring a more my-way-or-the-highway approach to women. Mr. Wrong is the kind of man who'll make you pay for every meal and turn you into his personal ATM. He's a cheap, unshaven, bottom-feeder who drowns his sorrows and does as he pleases, rarely—if ever—taking you into consideration. He also kisses like a bloated trout and wouldn't know romance if

Audrey Hepburn beat him over the head with her best Chanel clutch.

If Mr. Wrong is anything, he's predictable. He's jealous, chauvinistic, and chances are he cares little about your wants, needs, feelings, reactions or anything that remotely resembles partnership. There's no yin and yang with this guy. His yang is a whacked-out mix of clueless vulgarity and Neanderthal nuances. Rest assured that every woman has, at least once in her dating career, been forced to deal with Mr. Wrong. They all tried. They seldom conquered. And there's no shame in that. Now forget about this petulant creature, strap yourself in the saddle, and venture off into the dating frontier. You've survived a few showdowns, and from here on out your journey can only get better.

The Bottom Line: He loves you not. Wasting more time on Mr. Wrong would be criminal, and chances are he already is.

81 to 128 points: Mr. Noncommittal

Commitment is the art of binding yourself to a goal. It could be as simple as becoming a better fly fisherman or as complex as building a skyscraper. Whatever undertaking individuals choose to do, the important thing is that they dedicate themselves and see it through from beginning to end.

Unfortunately, that's not the case with your potential mate. Dealing with Mr. Noncommittal is like riding a rollercoaster twenty-four hours a day. He says he'll do something, but he rarely does. He promises you the moon and sends you a meteor. Try as he may, this guy of yours can be an emotional, physical, mental, and social nightmare, and no matter how hard *you* try—you're damned if you do and damned if you don't.

Non-Com boys tend to be immature about most things and constantly wobble between utter cluelessness and staunch opinions. This is the kind of guy who'd invite his ex-wives to your surprise birthday party and later wonder why you're a tad upset. He will comfort you, but he'll likely commit the same offense without hesitation. Non-Com boys can also switch gears, from jealous lover to chatterbox to drama queen in the blink of an eye, and no woman who ever hopes for a moment's peace needs a man like that.

Tragic though it may be, it's clear that your fellow is fond of you, but not for the reasons you'd like him to be. He does express affection, but usually when he's in the mood or when it's to his benefit. On occasion Mr. Noncommittal can find his way to becoming a solid partner, but it's a crapshoot. If you're a gambling woman, odds are you won't find true happiness with a guy who won't place a significant bet.

The Bottom Line: He likes you, but it's inevitable that he'll sit on the fence forever until the next best thing comes along and distracts him. Take heart in knowing that it's possible he could be committed—but not in a good way.

129 to 176 points: Mr. Limbo

Imagine what it would be like to live in a complete state of oblivion, enveloped in a mist of idle fantasy, cryptic events, and scattered emotions. That is what life is like for Mr. Limbo, and if your guy is hanging in the balance you're all too aware of his tendency toward escapism. It would be easy to justify a man such as this with excuses ranging from individuality to creativity, but you know better. Limbo man is a self-absorbed creature who more often than not pays little regard to your feelings in most situations.

Your limbo lover is trapped between alternately committing himself to you or running for cover. Sometimes he has the ability to communicate and you think you understand him, but then he goes an entirely different direction and you haven't a clue where he's headed. He'll spend weeks playing couch potato, and then he'll spend weeks at the gym. One weekend he'll party till he passes out, the next weekend he's in bed by ten.

Limbo guys tend to turn inward when the going gets tough. On the high side, they can sometimes be sweet and caring and show potential for becoming a proper mate. On the low side, they can teeter between daft and egomaniacal. If you're going to put your time and energy into Mr. Limbo, you've got your work cut out for you. More than likely, he's not a man who will change easily and not just for anyone—even you. So think long and hard before you take on this guy because you may find that he drags you down into oblivion.

The Bottom Line: Mr. Limbo is falling for you, but he's confused. The issue of whether he will or won't commit to anyone other than himself is a dating debacle. Your heart may be an open book, but the writing is on the wall.

177 to 224 points: Mr. Tolerable

Pretend for a moment that choosing a guy was like attending a police lineup. A half dozen manly specimens, each holding up a sign describing their personality and listing their classification, stare blankly at a two-way mirror hoping to get chosen by a buxom blonde.

Would any self-respecting woman in her right mind let out an excited gasp and scream: "That's him! He's the one I want . . . Mr. Tolerable!"

Unfortunately, though he's rarely chosen, many women do end up with this middle-of-the-road rogue and all his half-hearted brilliance. Now, that's not to say that Mr. Tolerable doesn't have potential; it's just that he often requires a lot of training, which can leave you more exhausted than exhilarated. If your guy falls into this category, he can be many different things. Tolerable men are the chameleons on the male dating scale. At times they can be aloof and other times they can be survivors. If your guy was unemployed, for example, he'd take whatever job he could to get by. But if you earn a higher salary than he does, he'd likely have a hissy.

On a personal level Mr. Tolerable can often be rational, but he usually fails to make the right decisions. When the two of you are together he's not a wholly generous man, so giving and sharing won't come to him naturally. In that regard he'll require nudging, and in the end you'll likely give much more than you receive. But any amount of time spent with Mr. Tolerable is never a waste, because he's the ideal benchmark test. Given his wide range of possible actions and reactions to any situation, it's easy for a woman to ascertain what she's truly looking for in a man.

If your guy is only tolerable, fear not dear lady, you'll now be able to look at a potential mate with better eyes, and it's only a matter of time before you spot someone who will adore you as much as you adore him.

The Bottom Line: He loves you more than you love him. Mr. Tolerable really isn't deserving of you and subconsciously you know it. You may think you won't find a better man, but you really shouldn't settle for less than you deserve—and you deserve better.

225 to 272 points: Mr. Maybe

Finding the right man is like going to the bakery. On one counter there are stacks of bread. There are loaves, rolls, baguettes, brioche, sourdough, rye, and sprouted wheat. They're stable, healthy, and wholesome. On the other counter are pastries. Petit fours, éclairs, donuts, *pan au chocolat,* cream puffs, and fruit tarts. They're light, sweet, and decadent. What do you choose? Do you go with a sturdy whole-wheat bread that keeps you steady or a delicate creampuff that gives you a rush?

If your man is Mr. Maybe, you've obviously walked out of the bakery with an armload of whole grain bread and a half dozen Krispy Kremes. Fellows who fall into the "maybe" category can provide a solid, healthy relationship, but they can also elicit that sinking drag you get from cupcake overload.

Mr. Maybe can have Jekyll-and-Hyde moments, but the way he copes with them is critical when it comes to ascertaining whether he's at the higher end of the potential scale or on the brink of becoming terminally tolerable.

Mr. Maybe has usually been burned, and he often comes with baggage and a host of wide-ranging opinions. As a partner your guy can probably be very agreeable, but his complacency can sometimes frustrate you. If you're going to stick with this guy, it's going to take time and effort. How much and how long is entirely dependent on whether he's willing to drop all pretense and start learning what it is to be a truly committed partner. So, the oven's turned on. Does he truly want to be a sourdough man, or is he content being a butter horn?

The Bottom Line: He loves you and he's trainable, but dedicating yourself to him is a question of whether or not you're willing to dedicate the time and energy it will take to elevate his love, companionship, and success quotients.

273 to 319 points: Mr. Potential

The moment a woman first lays eyes on a man who draws her attention, she asks herself three simple questions. *Is he single? Is he sane? Does he have potential?* If the answer to two out of the three is yes, then he's a man worth considering. The extent of his sanity is typically the toughest part of the equation to ascertain, but a single bloke who appears to have potential is a risk most of us are willing to take. And we do—all the time.

If your fellow is Mr. Potential, then you have a lot to be thankful for. Men of his caliber are generally thoughtful and caring individuals who often go the extra mile to bring joy and class to both of your existences. They are passionate souls who rarely overlook your wants and needs on emotional, physical, and spiritual levels, and while they do have their ups and downs, they can usually bounce back with relative grace and aplomb. If they have a fault, it's that sometimes they need a gentle nudge in order to keep focused on a certain activity or reassurance if they start feeling insecure.

A man who has the potential to be the cream in your coffee is worth fighting for. He'll certainly have opinions and will no doubt exhaust himself trying to keep life on an even keel, but his strong sense of duty, protocol, and his devotion to making things work—especially during rough patches—will make him a solid partner. Mr. Potential is a painting in progress, but his colors are true, and his portrait will be made all the better as he recognizes his true image and works to improve his form. He may not yet be a masterpiece, but if he's yours, he's certain to be a collector's item.

The Bottom Line: He definitely loves you, but on occasion he falters. He's a man with a lot of potential and he could eventually be your Mr. Right, it's simply a matter of whether or not he can learn to be a better man. Overall, the outlook is good, so keep the faith!

320 to 400 points: Mr. Right

When it comes right down to it, is it really and truly possible to find the perfect man? Not just any man. One who is compatible with you in all aspects of spiritual and physical life. One who complements you in every possible way. One who doesn't do a single thing that remotely irks you. Can that really happen? If you're laughing hysterically right now, it's for good reason. Get real. There's no such thing as the perfect man any more than there is the perfect woman. They're mythical creatures. You can get in the ballpark, but it would be utterly naive to think that your man is Mr. Perfect.

That said, it would appear that your fellow is pretty darn close, and the best news is that he loves you heart and soul. On the whole you're a lucky gal. Your gent is thoughtful, intelligent, caring, and well grounded, and he takes great pride in your accomplishments as well as his own. He's ambitious and career-minded, but he's careful to balance work and play so as not to be consumed by any extreme. Mr. Right is dependable to a fault and doesn't need to work hard within his circle of friends and family members because they all adore him as much as you do.

On an emotional level, your guy is generous. He's always sharing his hopes, dreams, fears, and opinions, and never hesitates to listen to yours. He loves to have a good time, but events are always sweeter if he can somehow add a personal touch or spoil you—not because he's showy, but because he wants to show you how much he cares and appreciates you. It's cliché to say that every woman dreams of finding her Mr. Right, but if this man is all he purports to be, you're one of the fortunate few who has found the best of the bunch. Congrats!

The Bottom Line: He loves you—a lot. There's little doubt that this man cares for you mind, body, heart, and soul. If you feel he's your soul mate, it's very possible you've made the right choice!